Llewellyn's
2014
Witches'
Companion

An Almanac for Everyday Living

Llewellyn's 2014 Witches' Companion

ISBN 978-0-7387-2157-6

Art Director: Lynne Menturweck
Cover art © Tim Foley
Cover designer: Lynne Menturweck
Designer: Joanna Willis
Editor: Andrea Neff

Interior illustrations:
Kathleen Edwards: 39, 42, 90, 93, 150, 153, 204, 208, 211, 258, 260
Tim Foley: 9, 11, 16, 62, 67, 77, 123, 125, 126, 147, 175, 177, 178, 213, 235, 239
Bri Hermanson: 20, 23, 70, 75, 131, 133, 135, 182, 185, 242, 245, 246
Jennifer Hewitson: 54, 57, 58, 111, 114, 117, 165, 167, 168, 170, 217, 220, 265, 266, 268
Christa Marquez: 31, 32, 34, 81, 82, 87, 140, 142, 145, 192, 194, 199, 249, 253
Rik Olson: 47, 50, 98, 100, 103, 104, 156, 159, 160, 225, 226, 229

Additional illustrations: Llewellyn Art Department

You can order Llewellyn annuals and books from New Worlds, Llewellyn's magazine catalog. To request a free copy of the catalog, call toll-free 1-877-NEW-WRLD, or visit our website at http://www.llewellyn.com.

Printed in the United States of America

Llewellyn Worldwide Ltd.
2143 Wooddale Drive
Woodbury, MN 55125-2989
www.llewellyn.com

Contents

Community Forum

Provocative Opinions on Contemporary Topics

Witchy Living

Day-by-Day Witchcraft

Witchcraft Essentials

Practices, Rituals & Spells

MELANIE MARQUIS

While it might seem counterintuitive to assume that taking more time for magick will actually create more time, that's exactly what happens when you bump ritual and spellwork to the top of your to-do list. Melanie Marquis shares some fun and easy ways to magickally carve out more time in your day.

ELIZABETH BARRETTE

Chalices, bowls, and cauldrons all represent the divine feminine, the Goddess. Elizabeth Barrette guides you in choosing the perfect tools to work your magick by explaining what each tool stands for and how its shape and material can contribute to the overall working.

DEBORAH BLAKE

Deborah Blake presents five of the most powerful and functional of all the gemstones used in magick today, plus how to select and care for them.

SUSAN PESZNECKER

Susan Pesznecker recommends taking a break from all the multitasking of our digital world and finding the quiet within ourselves—the place from which intention and magick spring.

THURI CALAFIA

What is dedication, anyway? And how does it differ from commitment? Thuri Calafia explores the issue of dedication to a spiritual path and presents a dedication ritual that she performs with her students.

Magical Transformations

Everything Old Is New Again

The Lunar Calendar

September 2013 to December 2014

Community Forum

Three Generations of Pagan

Kerri Connor

I was Pagan long before I knew what Pagan was.

Though I was born and raised in an Evangelical Protestant church, I had never felt comfortable in that environment. I heard and saw too many things that didn't make sense, left me with a bad feeling, or just made me feel like I was surrounded by hypocrites. I was expected to listen, not question—and to do what I was told, but not do what I saw others around me doing. It was frustrating and disheartening. I continued to go to church as I was told, but I never felt good about it.

One day when I was sixteen years old, my friends and I were hanging out at Wendy's house. She pulled out her Ouija board, and we began trying it out. We soon discovered that certain combinations of people worked better on the board than others. We didn't know anything at the time about mediums or channelers. What we did know was that we were communicating with what claimed to be the spirits of loved ones we had lost.

In order to preserve integrity, we did not allow anyone to work on the board while communicating with a loved one of their own. We wanted to make sure no one was moving the planchette to give more accurate answers.

What we found was that the vast majority of the information we received was correct. The people working the board had no clue what the answers were to some of the questions that were asked, and yet almost every verifiable answer was correct.

During this session, one of the spirits we communicated with was my own mother, who had passed away when I was eight. We began asking questions that were unverifiable, such as, "Are the streets of heaven really paved with gold?" Such questions may seem silly, but the answers we received were surprising. Though we were told that heaven was beautiful and full of nature, we were also told that it wasn't like we thought it was. We couldn't get answers to some of our questions. Many of the answers were things like, "You aren't ready to know" and "Some things must be experienced to be believed."

These words opened a new world to many of us who were in that room that day. We began doing a lot of research. Our town library didn't have any information—shocking, I know. We went to the next town over, with a much larger population, and started by re-searching Ouija and then spirit boards.

Of course a lot of information we found at first said that the board was the work of the Devil and was controlled by demons, but we knew it didn't feel that way. So we kept digging.

Eventually we found information on Spiritualism, which then led us to Witchcraft and Wicca, and finally to all sorts of different aspects of Paganism and Neopaganism.

Some of my friends freaked out and ran back to their Christian ideas and churches, but Wendy and I both continued reading, learn-ing, and evolving. We ended up going our own separate ways even-tually, both physically and spiritually.

I had to work pretty hard to learn about Paganism. In the mid-1980s, there weren't a whole lot of books available, especially where I lived. In our quaint "Christian" town, there were no bookstores other than the Christian bookstore. There weren't any metaphysical shops, and there also wasn't any Internet access to look up informa-tion or to connect with others of like mind.

My "training" took place in what I could find and in the natu-ral world around me. As I grew older, more information became available. The Internet was soon in everyone's home, making a world of information available to those who knew how to find it.

My beliefs and ideas also changed over the years. While I started off learning about and practicing Wicca, there were some aspects I did not feel comfortable with. I ended up making a drastic change and began working with Egyptian gods and goddesses instead. Finally, I began feeling a strong draw to my Irish roots, and my practice turned to Druidry, where I have been happy and content ever since. The group I run—The Gathering Grove—does not claim any one pathway. Instead, we are a mixed bunch that share and combine some of our beliefs. We tend to keep our public rituals on the more generic side, working simply with "God" or "Lord" for our masculine deity, while the feminine divine is known as "Goddess" or "Lady." In our private rituals, we use whichever pantheon we subscribe to individually.

One idea of mine that has really changed over the years has to do with raising children in the same faith you practice. When I first began learning about Paganism (and many years into it actually), it was a big no-no to raise your children in your own faith. The consensus was to allow your child to grow and then experience religion on their own terms when they were older and capable of making thier own choices. There was to be no interference with "free will." This also meant that a whole lot of children were growing up with no type of spirituality whatsoever.

> **When I first began learning about Paganism, it was a big no-no to raise your children in your own faith…. This meant that a whole lot of children were growing up with no type of spirituality whatsoever.**

Since my parents were still very active in their church, and also very active in my children's lives, my children ended up being brought up rather similar to how I had been. My parents would take them to church, and when they spent the summers together, after my parents moved to a different state, they would attend Sunday school and vacation Bible school throughout their visits. They had religion, but no real spirituality in their lives.

Eventually I realized that even though popular opinion said I should not share my beliefs with my children, by not doing so, they were being exposed only to the beliefs of those people who were indeed sharing. This didn't sit too well with me, so when my twins were about twelve and their little brother ten, I began sharing bits and pieces of my faith with them.

Eventually I realized that even though popular opinion said I should not share my beliefs with my children, by not doing so, they were being exposed only to the beliefs of those people who were indeed sharing. This didn't sit too well with me ...

I didn't sit them down and say, "Okay, kids, Mom is Pagan and this is how it has to be." Instead, I introduced them to concepts. I emphasized nature and how they should try to incorporate nature into their lives, and how they should respect and revere all life around them.

I taught them about karma, and how you should treat others the way you want to be treated. I explained that what goes around, comes around—and often comes back worse than it was sent out.

I taught them that everything has a counterpart—light/dark, male/female, good/bad—and that we need both together. One cannot exist in a balanced universe without the other.

Books such as Amber K's *Pagan Kids' Activity Book* and Kristin Madden's *Pagan Homeschooling* were good starting points for me to teach my kids about the Lord and Lady.

I found other resources, including the SpiralScouts program, and we started our own hearth for our family. It wasn't easy, though. While some people believed it was perfectly fine to raise your children as Pagans (hence the resources we could find), many people still believed it was wrong and interfering with the child's free will.

I felt, and still do feel, that by *not* teaching our children our beliefs, we are doing both them and ourselves a huge disfavor. Though my own local community was supportive in my decision to educate my children, I had belonged to several online communities where people made it known that they did not agree with my choices. Imagine being condemned by Pagans for teaching your own children about Paganism!

Eventually, as the group I started in 2003 began to grow, my children began to want to be more and more involved with the rituals. Today, they are all adults, and two of the three are regular members of The Gathering Grove. The third comes to ritual when he can, and though he is Pagan-friendly, he does not claim any one religion for himself.

My daughter, Krystle, who is a member of The Gathering Grove and also the North Eastern Illinois chapter of the Witch Hat Society, has a child of her own now. My granddaughter, Kahlen, may still be just a little tyke, but she has been to rituals already. At her first ritual, The Grove blessed her, with everyone taking turns to welcome her into our group and into our lives.

By eight months old, she had her own drum and "joined" our drum circle as well as a drum circle at a local metaphysical store. Her life so far has been different from what her mother's was as a child, and will continue to be so. Right from the very start, she will grow up knowing of a God and a Goddess. She will grow up with a love of nature and the natural world around her. Yes, she may decide to go off in search of a different path when she is older, but for now she is being raised in a world where she will not have to search for information on Paganism. Today there is much more available for children, both younger and older children. She can even learn her ABCs in a Pagan way: "A" is for athame now, not just alligator!

While in some circles raising a child Pagan is still taboo, it is becoming more and more acceptable. The concept that it was *not* okay to raise a child in this manner was NEOpagan, with an extreme emphasis on the "neo" part. Our Pagan ancestors didn't question whether they should teach their offspring their ways. It was always done and it was considered natural. Not raising your child in your belief system was unheard of. It helped to ensure survival of the tribe or clan *and* their beliefs. Yet this was something that many modern Pagans didn't find to be an appropriate part of their lifestyle. You don't find Christian families trying to decide whether or not their children should be raised in the family faith—it is simply done.

Krystle decided to raise Kahlen this way because she wants Kahlen to grow up well rounded and worldly. She feels it is important for Kahlen to experience Paganism so when the time is right, Kahlen will have the knowledge to choose what path is right for her.

A large part of the reason I decided to go ahead and raise my children with a deep understanding of Paganism was because it was the way things used to be done. It's traditional. As someone with Irish blood running through my veins, I feel a strong call to all things Celtic. I am proud of that Irish blood, and I want my children to be proud of it also. I have always felt that when we hide a part of ourselves, it is often done out of shame or embarrassment—and even when it isn't, others still perceive that that is why we are hiding something. The more proud Pagans we have standing up for themselves and their rights, the easier it will be for others to stand with them.

Someday, perhaps, we won't be concerned with what religion or form of spirituality someone practices and there truly will be equal rights for all, but that day isn't here … yet.

Kerri Connor *is the author of* The Pocket Spell Creator, The Pocket Guide to Rituals, The Pocket Idiot's Guide to Potions, Goodbye Grandmother, *and* Spells for Tough Times *and is the former editor of* The Circle of Stones Journal. *Kerri is the High Priestess of The Gathering Grove and has been practicing her craft for 26 years. She dances under the moon in rural Illinois.*

Illustrator: Tim Foley

When Pagans Get Old

Boudica Foster

I hobbled around the house yet again, a victim of my own stupidity. I contemplated once again the move my husband and I were making, and wondered if the doctors who had lately become dependent on our old-age accidents would be able to continue making a living once we were gone.

See, we had spent the past twelve years in the house of our Pagan dreams, complete with five sustainable acres for food, and we were giving it up and returning to urban America. We finally figured out that the keeping of the land, being stewards of the land, is for

We finally figured out that the keeping of the land, being stewards of the land, is for the young and foolish, not the older and wiser.

the young and foolish, not the older and wiser.

That is not to say we weren't young and foolish once. When we bought this house, we were young. Okay, we were younger. Well, we were younger than we are now, by about twelve years. We had this Pagan dream: to live on the land, to live with it and sustain ourselves on our very own "homestead." We had a lot of work to do those first years, and I was pretty glad we were still capable of doing lots of heavy work back then.

We had dreams of living on our own food, living with a small footprint, recycling and reusing what we could to be as Earth-friendly as we could. Looking back now, that was pretty damn ambitious for a couple of middle-aged city kids. We got jobs, we cleaned up the property, and we went to bed exhausted each and every night. We spent a lot of time working on this place. Looking back now, I remember what a mess it was when we moved in. Now we can call it "park-like" in the property description for the sales brochure for this place.

See, as we got older, we thought we could take it easier and eventually retire with little or no effort on our part—not! We may want to retire, but the land does not. It keeps going, no matter what you do. Don't weed it for a month or two, and it returns to its original state. It is now time to leave this place to the next generation.

My hubby has learned to swing an ax and use a chainsaw and a wood splitter. He has also ripped his rotator cuffs. His arms are not as limber as they used to be. He has taken a couple of spills as well, and he aches from time to time when he has overdone it or the weather changes. But the fireplace is not going to burn if we don't

have wood. And to heat this house, while it's not entirely without insulation, still costs more than two retired Pagans could afford. Retirement means less income, and in an area where jobs are few and far between, we need to take what Mother Nature gives us and cut it up and burn it. And this author is not very good at using a chainsaw.

I've broken my foot twice, ripped up my knee in ice falls, and am hobbling around with an injured foot again. No, mine isn't work-related. I just keep falling down the damn stairs in the house due to my own stupidity. Yes, stairs can be just as dangerous as a falling tree limb. Then again, I am not known for doing graceful well.

As both of us are approaching sixty, these injuries are becoming a concern. We can't afford more injuries like this. There comes a time in everyone's life when we have to say we have done all we can, it's time to move on.

There is a lot of work to do for a two-story house and four-plus acres of property. While it may not sound like much, most of it is trees, grass, and wet. It requires constant landscaping—cutting grass, trimming, tree maintenance and water maintenance. We have a river, a creek, and a pond. Yes, those need maintenance as well. And for those of you who want to keep it natural, there is a price to pay for that. Mosquitoes are a major issue here, as are ticks. With all the diseases here from these two sources alone, we made a decision long ago to reduce that risk factor. That takes work. Oh, and by the way, none of what we do has discouraged any of the wildlife here. We have deer, turkey, coyote, eagles, hawks, heron, raccoon, possum, and more. They all seem to settle into the property here and rest when passing through. None of them seems to mind our landscaping. Rather, it seems to signal a rest stop for them, and we appreciate seeing them come to relax on their journeys through our space.

We have put up with the forces of nature over the years. We had a "wind" event a few years ago. It took down some massive, old trees all over the property. Mother Nature takes out the old to make way for the new. In the process, we got firewood for a couple of winter seasons. We were very fortunate that none of those trees landed on our house. So, hubby takes to cutting the downed trees, and in the process, as he moved one piece out of the way to cut further, thwap! A branch that had been bent back and held down by that piece of tree sprung back, hitting my poor hubby in the face. Thank goodness he was wearing safety glasses, or it could have been worse. He did suffer a broken nose, which sprouted the bonus black eye. He could have lost his eye, or worse. We laugh about it now, and we consider it lucky it wasn't worse. But if that happened now, it could result in more serious injuries. He just isn't as fast as he was then.

Moving rocks used to be so easy. Well, the rocks are now getting bigger, heavier, and impossible to move—just because we are not as agile as we used to be. And even after twelve years, the land still has rocks. They range from small and annoying to huge and immovable. And the immovable ones are always in the middle of whatever project needs to be done.

As for our gardens, that has been a learning process as well. Heck, we live in the middle of farm country, so this had to be an ideal place for gardening. Our first gardens were failures, as we moved them from place to place around the property. Either not enough sun, too much sun and no available water to irrigate, or animals. I remember my first lettuce patch. It sprouted up, all the tender green shoots, and the day I went to pick my first salad, some animals had had a buffet the night before. It was picked clean. We ended up converting a flowerbed at the house edge into our garden. Close to the house, the deer did not venture. We at least get veggies from it now.

We learned the value of rotating crops. We learned that not everything will grow everywhere. And we learned to identify poison ivy, which will grow anywhere. Digging out weeds requires a careful eye, or you end up with a terrible case of poison ivy. Trust me; I have had firsthand experience.

We didn't want to use insecticides. That was a major concern for us. So we deal with bugs. Tobacco worms, Japanese beetles, grubs. And weeds. Bending over the garden daily results in visits to the chiropractor. But in the end, it has been satisfying. We have our own food on our table. Nothing is more satisfying.

Digging soil every spring is not something we can continue to do. And no, a rototiller is not the answer. Remember my mentioning the rocks? I will allow you to use your imagination in regard to the one and only rototiller we rented. Not pretty.

And then there is the wildlife. I mentioned the deer. They tend to wander around the property and relax—and munch on whatever they can get into when you are not looking. Wild turkeys are interesting when they are not chasing the cats. Coyotes are dangerous. And yes, we have coyotes here. Raccoons are just plain nasty. But the worst? Skunks! Young skunks are unpredictable. We have not had a direct run-in with them, but it is only a matter of time. We have had five young skunks and their mom running around the property, and that is just scary. One wrong move and you could have a stink bomb of massive proportions. The wildlife is wonderful here, but we have great respect for it all. I think, however, that I would like to move to an area where we do not have to keep that as a major concern.

The house is a topic all on its own. From scrambling up to the roof to clear debris and check the shingles, to making repairs on the exterior porches and gutters, we have done it all. We even had bees move into the walls and find a way into the house one year. Bee stings were common that year. Thank goodness we are not allergic.

It isn't realistic to expect that you can continue to be superman or superwoman. We come home from work, work on the property or house, and fall asleep waiting for dinner to cook. And we use a microwave! I really want to retire in a few years and have no intention of handing over my paycheck each week to contractors to do the work, or spend weekends with hammer and hoe.

So, as we were painting downstairs yet again, standing on a stool to reach the upper trim, I stretched the muscle in my foot a bit too far and now am limping. At least last time I did it dancing around on St. Paddy's Day. No such great excuse this time.

We are also not close to the city, but about twenty minutes out. And we are not exactly close to our neighbors in any way, shape, or form. I took a dive on the ice last winter and ended up on crutches. But I was home alone at that point, and there was no one to help me once I fell. I will not discuss how I managed to make it back to the house, but I will not go through that again. I laugh about it now, but it wasn't funny then.

The dream house has been a learning experiment, and one that I am glad I have had the opportunity to live for the past twelve years. I have had the best time with my husband doing what we have done. We are leaving this place better than we found it. It is beautiful, and the property is still treed, but well kept and natural. But I am, at heart, a city girl. And hubby is somewhere

I have had the best time with my husband doing what we have done. We are leaving this place better than we found it…. But I am, at heart, a city girl.

between the country and the city. I would like to walk sidewalks again; I still want a green backyard, but with less maintenance.

As I slowly pack up all our belongings, I contemplate what it means to be Pagan, and to be getting old. While I really want to continue this lifestyle, one that we are both deeply in love with, we need to be realistic. There comes a point when we need to realize that it is time to let go. Time to start walking that path again and move on. Time to take inventory of health and the benefits of living on the land as an older person. There is no shame in moving on. I will cherish the tomatoes, as they will be the last ones from this garden. I have zucchini and beans and basil. I will not be canning any of this, but will stuff myself or give away what we do not use. Next year, patio tomatoes on my back porch will be my garden. And a pot of basil.

Boudica Foster *co-owns* The Wiccan/Pagan Times, *an online Pagan e-zine, with her husband. She is a native New Yorker who had been displaced to the wilds of mid-Ohio, but now resides in suburban Pennsylvania. Boudica has self-published one spell e-book and a basic book on Reiki and is almost done with a second spell e-book and a fictional piece. She donates time to other websites that promote Pagan paths, writing, and self-publishing and assists other writers in achieving their own goal of writing and self-publishing. She is a working Witch of over 35 years and now prefers the solitary experience and her own personal spirituality. She lives with her husband of many years and four cats.*

Illustrator: Bri Hermanson

Burning Ourselves at the Stake: The Confusing Madness of "Witch Wars"

Michael Furie

Every so often a "Witch War" erupts, and whether it be some local conflict or a controversy that gets nationwide attention (or beyond), it is a phenomenon that creates a large amount of division and hurt among those directly involved and a great deal of confusion for the rest of us left standing on the outside wondering which way to turn. Everything from the proprietors of local competing Witch shops badmouthing each other in an attempt to drive the other out of business (which happened in a nearby town several years ago), to Internet bloggers voicing disgust at and trying to discredit prominent Witches either for being "too public" or for using terms or practices that they deem inferior or inappropriate—it all creates so much tension and discomfort that I feel it threatens to wreak havoc on our still struggling community.

I have read some incredibly hateful things written in online book reviews about well-known Pagan authors that many times appear to be quite obviously written solely from personal bias and rarely even address specific issues about the book they are supposed to be reviewing. And social media seems to be rife with "Witch War Madness" as well. Recently, I saw a photo post of a prominent Wiccan author's personal altar loaded with angry accusations of materialism and lack of spirituality from some random person who didn't even know the author. Some of the author's friends came to their defense, stating that the author had been collecting those items over many years and that they were in fact, quite a spiritual person. I noticed that the author did not personally respond to any of the hateful comments, apparently taking the high road of not wanting to engage in public bickering. But, I digress.

There are so many different manifestations of Witch Wars, and it seems that very little is needed to spark one, but I've been considering the overall subject of Witch Wars in general and I have noticed a few things. Most of the controversies and turmoil that are sparked by Witches of differing philosophies seem to stem from personal (as opposed to religious) prejudices, phobias, or apparently opposing beliefs. Rather than seek compromise, walk away, or agree to disagree, both sides choose to argue and escalate the conflict into all-out war, with name-calling, rumor-mongering, and hate being thrown around and diminishing both sides' credibility. I feel that this is a dangerous practice that only serves to undermine the still fragile reputation of all Witches in the public eye.

As a practice, Witchcraft has still only just started to be seen as a "legitimate" path among outsiders and continues to suffer smear campaigns and slander from other, more dominant religions. As public Witches (those of us who are), it is vital that we show a public face of truth, unity, integrity, wisdom, and credibility. When we get mired in petty bickering and mudslinging amongst our own people, how can we ever expect to enjoy mainstream acceptance from those of other faiths? As private Witches, it is imperative that we have within ourselves and our practice those qualities of truth, unity, integrity, wisdom, and credibility so that we can be a positive influence both in our lives and in the lives of others.

As private Witches, it is imperative that we have within ourselves and our practice those qualities of truth, unity, integrity, wisdom, and credibility so that we can be a positive influence both in our lives and in the lives of others.

I do understand that people have different viewpoints and different practices, traditions, gods, values, and ethical codes and that we can't all be expected to get along at all times just to avoid looking bad in the eyes of others. That was, however, my first point, because I think it's a very valid one and worthy of consideration by all Witches, regardless of tradition. Another and much more personally important reason for sidestepping any attempt by others to pull you into a Witch War is that our religion (and our magic) is one of individuality and personal experience. The truth and beauty found in the Craft is (though it can be shared with others both ritually and anecdotally) solely a solitary experience, shared with no one else except your deities. Even when working with other Witches in a coven or open circle, the inner connections, feelings, and transformations that occur are highly personal feats, and one person's experience of powerful ritual could be another's experience of personal blockage or marginal connection. It must be realized that not everyone perceives things in the same way, and try though we may by carefully cultivating the group mind (in coven and circle workings), each person sees with separate eyes and feels with a separate heart.

What the heck does that have to do with angry Witches? Well, I have a theory about the root causes of so-called Witch Wars. As we grow in our journey as Witches and our magic deepens, if we work with other Witches, we cultivate an unspoken bond and a type of telepathic group mind when in circle. Whether we work with others or not (this isn't a treatise on coven work), as we advance in our Witchcraft, we do develop an expanded consciousness and a psychically sensitive nature. This, of course, is perfectly natural as we learn to connect with the Gods and work with life energy. Since most of you know this, the only reason I bring it up is to point out three things:

1. There are people trying to practice who have not felt the transformation of the Craft.

2. The Witches who have been transformed through our practice are more sensitive to their surroundings than most people.

3. No matter how far into our practice we are—newbie, initiate, advanced, or elder—we are *all* human beings, and as such, are very capable of making mistakes.

Looking at the first one, I think that the majority of people instigating the Witch War conflicts are people who haven't been properly taught how to experience the Mysteries and transformation of Witchcraft. When people feel that they are unworthy, a reaction seems to be to "convert" others to their way of thinking in order to reinforce the belief in their own mind. We've seen this so often in other religions. How many ministers of other religions have stood up and proclaimed themselves to be enlightened, holy, and chosen to determine other people's spiritual worth, while at the same time they are sneaking around with prostitutes or embezzling money from their organization? This is a phenomenon to which we, as Witches, need not subscribe.

Ours is a practice (a craft, a religion, and an art) that is meant to celebrate our individuality and promote personal experience. It is *so* crucial that we each feel what we practice. When we merely go through the motions of ritual and don't experience the connection and energy that the ritual is meant to celebrate, a sense of hollowness results. I know this; I've experienced it. Witchcraft has always been in my life, and I knew bits and pieces of lore and magic but was left unaware of how to practice. When I first started trying to actually practice, I had a lot to learn and eagerly gobbled up every bit of information I was told and read every book I could get my hands on. Though I read and "knew" a great deal about the Craft and "practiced" ritual often, I really didn't feel much of anything other than the yearning I had always felt and hoped that fully embracing Witchcraft would finally assuage. Eventually, I solved the problem and deepened in my practice. The problem: I read a lot of books and listened to a lot of people, but I didn't really do what they said. I thought that an "intellectual understanding" of what I assumed was the teacher's point was reason enough to skip the exercise and move on to the next step. What I failed to realize was that intellectual understanding is only one facet of learning Witchcraft and is not the part that stirs the soul. The other facets of learning are emotional and spiritual, and these can only be utilized through the experience of the exercise.

The reason I share this personal snippet of my life is that it seems as though a great many of our kind are suffering from a type of "spiritual malnourishment" due to a lack of understanding of how to practice the Craft. The hollowness that I felt when my efforts went unrewarded fueled feelings of inferiority, doubt, confusion, and (I hate to admit) jealousy of my more gifted peers; I assumed that I was somehow lacking in potential, rather than realizing that I wasn't truly learning Witchcraft correctly. Feeling isolated and inferior is a difficult position to be in for anyone, but especially so for someone who is supposed to be learning how to open up spiritually and connect with energies and beings on many levels.

I've never been the type of person to lash out at others when I feel upset. I wasn't raised in one of the dominant religions and as such do not relate to that dogma, but many people coming to Witchcraft were raised in one of the dominant faiths. In many other religions, it seems to be believed that there is "only one way" to do things, only one way to relate to the world. If you were brought up to believe that there is only one way to do something and you were unsuccessful using that method, where would that leave you?

For many, it seems to leave them feeling frustrated and betrayed. When feeling like this, it is only natural to lash out and try to find fault with others' practices. It is my feeling that this is the secret "why" behind many Witch Wars: poor souls stuck in technicalities and intellectual confusion, trying to assert some form of Witchcraft dogma where none exists. There are so many Witches in the world who haven't been properly nurtured and guided and taught to release the concepts of dogma and drudgery and shown how to truly experience the beauty and wonder of life. The secret solution to this is knowledge—the knowledge that Witchcraft is a religion/practice based on experience. You have to be an active participant in order to receive the benefits and beauty of this path. Practice makes perfect, after all.

My second point is that the Witches who have been transformed by our practice are more sensitive to their surroundings than most people. How this relates to Witch Wars is that when we feel that

someone is in pain or is lost, we tend to relate to them on a deeper level than mere surface sympathy. Many times, the desire to help those in need can lead us to give too much of ourselves—too much time, money, effort, or (more relevant to this article) personal information. There is danger in indiscriminately helping people in need.

Doesn't that sound awful? I feel bad for saying it, but it's true. Sometimes the emotional turmoil felt by somebody in pain overwhelms our senses and drowns out the little nagging voice that warns, "Don't trust this person." I'm not saying don't help people; don't give of yourself in service; don't reach out to others in need. I'm not saying that at all. I'm just saying that we need to keep in mind that our connection to others is a double-edged sword, and we need to maintain a certain detached, impartial perspective.

When others (strangers, friends, family, etc.) come to us seeking spiritual guidance or magical advice or, more often than not, ask us to "cast a spell" for them, we need to step back and evaluate their motives and spiritual condition. We, as Witches, mustn't allow ourselves to be drawn into other people's drama unnecessarily. To let ourselves be placed in the middle of someone else's battles is a diffusion of our power. An example: A man asks you to cast a spell to "reveal a liar" because he is certain that his wife is cheating, but meanwhile, he has secrets that he'd rather keep hidden. You cast the spell and all his secrets come out and he is publicly humiliated. In anger, he chooses to speak out against you, saying you're an evil Witch who "hexed" him and "it's all your fault." This example is a bit dramatic, but you see my point, right? It is so easy to be labeled "the problem" by people seeking a quick defense of their own misdeeds.

We need to be very sure, through our own detached intuition, divinations, and common sense, that we are helping someone worthy of our efforts when we offer assistance. This is primarily a problem for the more public Witch, but can still be an issue for any of us when we share our truth with others. We must be very sure of whom we trust and make sure they are deserving of such an honor. Anything less leaves us vulnerable to chaos, slander, and undo ridicule.

My third point is that, no matter how far into our practice we may be, we are all human and capable of making mistakes (and being petty). This aspect of Witch War wackiness usually manifests in the curious exercise of tradition bashing. Being a Witch means, among other things, that we acknowledge our individuality and realize that there are many paths to the Divine, and yet a lot of us seem to delight in picking

apart the Craft traditions of other Witches. This phenomenon has fascinated me for a long time, especially considering that the core of Witchcraft always remains the same, regardless of tradition. An unfortunate manifestation of tradition bashing is when "Traditional Witches" bash modern Witches mercilessly.

In truth, I am a Traditional Witch, but so what? It doesn't mean anything in the grand scheme of things other than what my own spiritual and magical experiences are to me. It doesn't make me better or worse than any other Witch out there. The same is true of all Witches of any sort; the only measure of our skill, practice, worth, power, magic, importance, etc., is within us and in our connection to the Gods. No one else can (or should) have the right to diminish our practice in any way. Even though we have clergy, the teachers of our ways can only facilitate and guide our learning, not learn for us or shape us into what they feel we need to be. No one should judge us but our own selves and the Gods.

I have never understood people bashing other people's traditions. No matter what, it's *all* Witchcraft. Whether ancient or modern, it's all interconnected. Ours is the only path that seems to have the problem of age-based "authenticity." In Christianity, no one ever seems to doubt that each is a member of a 2,000-year-old faith, even though individual denominations may be only a hundred years old or less. They realize that the age of the belief is what counts; why don't a lot of us realize that too? The truth of the matter is that Witchcraft is an ancient practice that has continued to grow and evolve as society has grown and evolved, for better or worse.

Also, so-called "modern" Witchcraft practices are actually ancient anyway. The only modern thing about them is how they are put together. Every Witch in the world is equal to every other Witch in the world, and any one of us who says differently should be held suspect in our eyes. Witchcraft is an acknowledgment, a celebration, and a connection to our true spirit; it is the realization that all things are directly connected to one other and that our place in this web of creation is one of power and strength. To participate in a Witch War is a diminishment of our power, and to start one is an affront to everything that Witchcraft is built upon, a total lack of inner Craft knowledge. We must all remember that we are truly directly connected to one other, and trying to tear someone else down tears us down just as much, maybe even more.

We must all remember that we are truly directly connected to one other, and trying to tear someone else down tears us down just as much, maybe even more.

I do understand that not all people claiming to be Witches are, in fact, credible, ethical Witches, and of course people should be warned away from charlatans or dangerous cults falsely claiming to be Witchcraft covens; but just because someone has a practice different from ours does not mean that they are a charlatan or part of a cult. It is very narrow-minded to think that a path is "valid" only if it happens to match our own. If we cannot respect the fact that other Witches have practices with which we may not agree, but that may be very effective for them, then we cannot truthfully state that we believe there are many paths to the Divine. The belief that no one path is right for everyone has been a hallmark of modern Paganism in all its forms and has been a very attractive aspect of our practices. While I have not heard any Witch or Pagan decry this belief, acting as though one path is more valid than another implies a "there's only one way" point of view. It worries me greatly when Craft elders espouse this view. Thankfully, it does not seem to occur very often, since it is (I feel) a very dangerous notion. When Craft elders can't grow beyond divisive views, they risk perpetuating them, and when this occurs, the education of the next generation of Witches could be irrevocably damaged. Instead of unleashing further hate, the rest of us as Witches need to focus on combatting any prejudice through example, by truly embracing and celebrating our differences as gifts from the Goddess.

Michael Furie *is from California. He has been a Witch for over 17 years. He enjoys cooking, reading, growing herbs, and studying herbalism, magic, and Irish lore.*

Illustrator: Christa Marquez

Lies My Magic Teacher Told Me

Elizabeth Barrette

The Pagan community relies a great deal on oral tradition. Yes, we have books now, which the earlier generations of contemporary Pagans did not. However, we still tend to pass along a great deal of knowledge from person to person, both individually and in groups. We have covens and classes and festivals. That makes it easy for ideas to remain in wide circulation even if they aren't completely true.

There are different types of incomplete truths. Sometimes an idea starts out as true, but circumstances change, and it doesn't apply the same way to the new situation. Sometimes it's true in some cases but not in others. Sometimes it's simply unfinished and there's a piece missing.

To work magic effectively and safely, you need to pay attention. By all means, read books and listen to teachers—but don't take anything for granted. Test out the magical principles presented to you and see if they actually work as advertised. Sometimes they will. Other times, you may notice discrepancies. Then it's up to you to refine your awareness until it matches what's actually going on. Here are some examples of this process.

"Ground to the Earth"

Grounding is the process of connecting personal energy to an outside energy source. This way, you can release excess energy if you are overloaded, or take in fresh energy if you are depleted. It also buffers your individual field against surges from the ambient field, much as a lightning rod safely directs lightning into the ground so it doesn't damage a building.

And there it is: *ground, grounding*. Magical vocabulary borrowed some terminology from electronics because different kinds of energy often work in similar ways. Because language influences thought, the term *grounding* makes us think of Earth. As it happens, the element of Earth is ideal for managing energy, and a majority of people find it easy to ground to Earth.

The catch is, there are people who can't do it that way. Because grounding to Earth is the only method described in most resources, and the only method many teachers know to present, these people often wind up thinking that they *can't ground at all*. This happens most often with people who connect strongly to Air, the opposite of Earth; but it can also happen with Fire or Water, because those elements also have mobile, flexible aspects unlike the stability of Earth.

The solution, then, is to "connect personal energy to a safe outside source." It can be any of the elements, and there are even other options beyond that. Try the most common option, Earth, first; and if that doesn't work, try others. Each has its own visualizations, such as a kite for Air, an anchored ship for Water, or a volcano for Fire. Experiment and find what works for you (or your students).

"An It Harm None, Do as Thou Wilt"

The Wiccan Rede is a core tenet of that religion. From there, it has spread throughout much of the modern Pagan movement. It often appears in truncated form, "Harm none," which is actually a different rule altogether.

As a conditional rule, the Wiccan Rede grants permission for all acts that cause no harm. That's useful, because a lot of other religions disallow things that are perfectly harmless yet are considered morally repugnant for some other arbitrary reason. In Wicca, harm is a meaningful moral threshold. Anything that doesn't cause harm is okay—for instance, loving someone of the same sex or having more than one lover at a time.

The catch is that the rule *doesn't address* harmful actions. Look closely. This is the difference between the long version and the short version. If your intended action harms nobody, you're free to do it according to Wiccan belief. But what if it does cause harm? How do you tell whether that's okay or not? "Harm none" is more akin to Buddhist tradition. It's not actually possible in mortal life—every time you blink, your eyelids kill microbes—so it's sometimes moderated to "Do least harm." That's still not the original Wiccan rule. There's a gap in it. Why? Wicca as a tradition doesn't really cover matters of war or self-defense. Different Pagan traditions emphasize different areas of expertise.

So if you're eclectic, as many people are these days, you can piece together an effective moral code by *combining* tenets from different paths. There are plenty of warrior traditions out there. Take Asatru, for example. "Have a fierceness of a wolf in protecting your own" appears in assorted versions. Consider that a wolf is gentle and loving with family and pack members, yet will fight to protect them and their territory if directly threatened. This draws on natural patterns, which is generally a good way to find a workable method.

There are, of course, many other traditions to consider. Look around and see what seems like a good match for you personally. It's possible to assemble a religion rather like mixing and matching puzzle pieces. You might be surprised what fits together.

"Always Work Deosil"

In Wicca and most other Pagan traditions, the direction of positive flow is *deosil*, also called sunwise or clockwise. People are customarily taught to cast circles and otherwise do magical work in this direction. The reverse rarely gets mentioned, except in the concept of "don't do things backward."

However, the opposite direction has its own uses even within the prevailing context. The direction of banishment and reversal is *tuathal*, also called moonwise, counterclockwise, or widdershins. Together, they make a very useful pair: clockwise for solar workings, summoning, and other positive applications, and counterclockwise for lunar workings, banishing, and other negative applications. A circle is usually taken down in the opposite order as it was cast, so the idea of counterclockwise motion is right there; but people rarely extend this awareness to the idea of casting counterclockwise for rituals in which that reversed energy would be useful throughout. This is not good if you're trying to make something *go away*.

Another thing to consider is that some traditions, such as Cherokee, customarily work counterclockwise. Sometimes it's about following the path of the moon, which creeps "backward" across the sky, appearing higher each night. Sometimes it matches the writing system, going left to right instead of right to left. There can be other reasons, too. Some left-handed practitioners find it easier to cast widdershins, which is fine for them.

One problem stemming from these perceptions is that deosil is "the right way" to do things, and that working widdershins is wrong or even evil. Sound familiar? That's exactly the kind of criticism hurled at Witchcraft from the outside. There's nothing evil or unnatural about a direction. It just depends on what you do with it. Whether it's the "right" direction depends on how well it matches the purpose of your current activity.

This is one of those cases where there isn't a single correct answer. Different cultures have different preferences in how they set the standard ways to do things. Magical correspondences align differently depending on what you want to accomplish in a given ritual. So when you see "always" or "never," don't take that for granted as an absolute rule. Think about it. Bear in mind that doing things another way may work better for certain goals, or that other people may follow another path. All of those things are okay.

"Crossing the Circle after It Has Been Cast Will Weaken It"

Rituals, spells, and other magical workings often begin by creating a boundary to contain sacred space within and keep unwanted influences out. This boundary almost always takes the shape of a circle, although other shapes have their uses. If you then need to have someone enter or leave the circle, you're supposed to "cut a door" to allow passage and then seal it up afterward. That tends to leave the circle a little more permeable.

This is basically a simplification. If something crosses the line of a cast circle, the most likely effect is a weakening of the circle. That's what happens for most people, if they don't take extra precautions to prevent it. However, there are exceptions. Some traditions consider that cats and small children, for instance, can cross a circle without disturbing it. Certain highly skilled practitioners may do the same, the magical equivalent of walking through a wall. Others may succeed in reforming the circle at the exact same strength as the original.

Why float this advice around, then? Because it discourages novices from attempting something that most people can't do safely or effectively. It also encourages people to plan ahead and make sure that everything needed for the ritual is in fact *inside the ritual area* before casting the circle. These points make for safer, more efficient ritual experiences.

A drawback is that it tends to discourage certain types of ritual activities and energy-handling skills. If you keep everyone inside the cast circle, then you lose some of the drama of having mythic figures move into and then out of the storyline, and so forth. If you don't try to match your energy signature to the circle so as to pass through it without disturbing it, you're not going to develop that skill. So if you want to explore those, you need a higher level of ability and more flexibility in ritual design.

Another option is simply to go around the whole issue. A circle may be cast in such as way as to allow transit without breaking it. Two good examples involve casting the circle through people's bodies, or casting it with an object, such as a ribbon, that can be lifted out of the way and then replaced. You just have to think outside the box—or in this case, the circle.

. . . .

Magic is a subtle and wonderful thing. Books are useful, and so are teachers. In the end, though, it comes down to what you observe and what you do. You're the one who has to figure out what works and what doesn't work for you. The same is true of covens and other magical groups. Don't believe something just because somebody important said it, especially if it doesn't explain all of your own experiences. Sometimes there is more than one right answer. Remember that even the "lies my magic teacher told me" can be learning experiences.

Elizabeth Barrette *has been involved with the Pagan community for more than 23 years. She served as managing editor of PanGaia for 8 years and dean of studies at the Grey School of Wizardry for 4 years. Her book* Composing Magic: How to Create Magical Spells, Rituals, Blessings, Chants, and Prayers *explains how to combine writing and spirituality. She enjoys magical crafts, historical religions, and gardening for wildlife. Visit her blog,* The Wordsmith's Forge *(http://ysabetwordsmith. livejournal.com), or her website,* PenUltimate Productions *(http://pen-ultimateproductions.weebly.com).*

Illustrator: Kathleen Edwards

Reclaiming the Word "Witch"

Cassius Sparrow

It wasn't so long ago that simply being a Witch was a most heinous crime, one that carried the strictest of penalties. Since then, times have changed and society has lessened its stigma on Witchcraft, but misinformation and negative portrayals of Witchcraft in the media have contributed to stereotypes and caricatures of Witches, Pagans, and Wiccans that are not only untrue, but are still quite harmful.

How often have you heard the term "Witch" used as an insult, or turned on your television to see Witches as villains cackling wickedly over a cauldron of

For Pagans and Wiccans to reclaim the word "Witch," we must first show the world what it means to be a Witch—an undertaking that is much simpler than you might initially believe.

bubbling, viscous liquid? Although interest in Paganism, Wicca, and other Earth-based religions has been on the rise, rarely do we see Witches portrayed in a truthful or even positive manner in popular media. That's not to say that it never happens; it just seems to be a rare occurrence.

For Pagans and Wiccans to reclaim the word "Witch," we must first show the world what it means to be a Witch—an undertaking that is much simpler than you might initially believe.

Write Letters to the Editors of Local Newspapers

The age-old tradition of writing letters to the editors of local newspapers is actually a very effective way of influencing public opinion. The most influential letters would be ones written around sabbats, especially Samhain and Yule, as these are holidays most commonly associated with Witches. Start by addressing and dispelling popular myths about the activities of Witches during the sabbats, and remember to be polite, as anything less will only hurt public opinion. Take the opportunity to explain how real Witches celebrate the various holidays, and include activities that you and your family participate in as well. Keep the letter brief, professional, and personal. If you feel comfortable enough to do so, identify yourself at the close of the letter. Having someone in the community who is open about Witchcraft will do a lot to help readers relate to the issue, as there is now a face to the name.

You can also volunteer to be interviewed for local interest pieces relating to Witchcraft. This is also especially effective around sabbats. As with editorial letters, remember to be professional and courteous. Keep the topic of the interview positive, be firm and polite when answering critical or negative leading questions, and request to see the interview before it is published, to ensure that none of your comments will be taken out of context.

Organize a Pagan Pride Day

If your city doesn't already have a Pagan Pride festival, consider organizing one. It may seem like a lot of work, but the effort put in will pay off in the end. Begin by setting up a committee of interested community members. You will need someone who is familiar with public relations to help get coverage from the local media. Involve community leaders and politicians as well, as they can help you promote the event. Set up a reasonable budget, and consider having local Pagan and Wiccan vendors at your event. Renting booths can help offset the

costs of setting up the festival.

Contact your city hall and police department regarding permitting and security requirements for holding the festival. Contact the health department as well, if you are planning to have food vendors. Choose a location for the event that offers amenities such as restrooms, shade, and places to sit, such as a local park.

Once you have a location and the necessary permits, it's time to start planning the Pride Day. Have a public ritual that includes everyone, even non-Witches. The more inclusive the event is, the more accepting the public will be toward it. Plan a charitable activity as well, such as a food drive or toy drive, or collect school supplies for children in need. Consider having an information booth, where people can ask questions about Paganism and Wicca, and learn more about Witchcraft as well. Remember to keep your Pagan Pride festival fun and family-friendly.

If your city already has a Pagan Pride Day, get involved with the event! Volunteer to work at the information booth, or suggest the creation of one. Become a vendor, play an instrument, or help organize the ritual. The most important step to gaining public awareness is to simply be involved.

Create an Open Group to Discuss Paganism and Wicca

Misconceptions come from misinformation, and most misinformed people do not know where to turn when they question those misconceptions. An open group can help get rid of negative stereotypes of Witches by creating a safe space for people to ask questions and learn more about Pagans, Wiccans, and Witches.

Libraries typically allow small groups to gather in meeting rooms. Just be sure to check with your local library about attendance limits and how early you would need to book the room. If your local library is out of the question, try contacting Unitarian Universalist churches in your area. Many have been known to host Pagan and Wiccan groups, as most Unitarian Universalists encourage diversity and different spiritual paths.

After you've secured a location for the group, start advertising. Create some flyers explaining what the group is about and where it will be located, and include the date and time. Be sure to mention that everyone is invited to join the group, regardless of religion. Consider posting advertisements on local online message boards.

Don't try to tackle hosting the group alone. Ask community members to volunteer to talk about their personal spiritual paths. Be sure to give equal attention to Paganism, Wicca, and other Earth-based paths. Breach the subject of Witchcraft with confidence and show that the word "Witch" is not a dirty word. Answer questions respectfully and keep the discussions family-friendly. You can host the group as a one-time event, or if it's successful enough, consider making it a monthly event.

Simply Talk to People

This might be the hardest action to take, especially if you're not publicly out of the broom closet, but the most effective way of changing minds is to simply talk to people about it. That doesn't mean you should aggressively pursue people to try to change their minds, but if the opportunity to talk to someone about Paganism, Wicca, or Witchcraft comes up, take it! Perhaps you overhear someone in a video rental store talking negatively about Witches in a movie. Politely introduce yourself and offer to clarify the situation. Tell them that movies often falsely portray Witches in an attempt to garner interest in the movie—especially in horror and science fiction—and that the truth about Witchcraft is actually much different. If they are interested, briefly explain to them that Witches are not inherently evil, that not all magick is "black magick," and if you can, give them a bit of insight into your own path. Be respectful of them if they are not interested in what you have to say.

If you have children in school, find out if their teachers will be discussing related topics, such as the history of Halloween or Arthur Miller's *The Crucible*, or other such subjects. If so, contact the school's principal and volunteer to give a talk about modern Witchcraft as related to the subject. Be aware that some parents will be averse to such a discussion, even in high schools, and that you may not be allowed to give a talk. If that is the case, remember to keep any appeals to such a decision polite and courteous. The worst-case scenario is that the school's principal will say no.

If you're a crafty person, you can make buttons or stickers with catchy sayings such as "Pagan and Proud" or "Ask Me Why I'm Wiccan." Wearing them on your clothes or accessories can open an opportunity for people to initiate a conversation with you in regard to Witchcraft. If you have created an open discussion group, invite them and their friends to join!

Changing the public perception of Witches starts with getting active in the community. By giving a positive face to Witchcraft, Pagans and Wiccans can show that negative portrayals of Witches are unfounded and should not continue just because popular media deems them to be all right. By reclaiming the word "Witch," we show that it's not an insult, and that Witchcraft is not to be feared as some dark and evil path to destruction, that it is a peaceful and welcoming spiritual path. Whether you single-handedly organize your city's first Pagan Pride Day, or simply take an opportunity to talk to your friends and neighbors about Paganism and Wicca, you're helping to raise awareness and tolerance in the community. Every action, no matter how small, is important so long as it is done in a friendly, polite, and respectable manner.

For More Information

The Pagan Pride Project, http://www.paganpride.org

Unitarian Universalist Association of Congregations, http://www.uua.org

Cassius Sparrow *is an Eclectic Pagan Witch, Tarot reader, author, and garden enthusiast. He is a devotee of both Hermes and Dionysos, and has been a practicing Pagan for over 10 years. He currently lives on the Gulf Coast of Florida with his darling wife and their cat, Zucca. In his free time, he can be found writing, baking, or working in his herb garden. Contact him at cassiussparrow@gmail.com.*

Illustrator: Rik Olson

Devil Take the Hindmost:
Adventures in the Black School

Linda Raedisch

Before there was Hogwarts, Brake-bills, or the Grey School of Wizardry, there was the Black School. From about the sixteenth to the early twentieth century, *Migratory Legend 3000: Escape from the Black School* (as the folklorists like to call it) was a staple of the European storyteller's repertoire. In the English-speaking world, ML 3000 was eventually eclipsed by ML 3020, familiar to most of us as *The Sorcerer's Apprentice*. Cracked stone floors and crooked steeples throughout England have been blamed on the actions of the demon unleashed by said apprentice.

Fantasy novelist Ursula K. Le Guin employed the motif in A *Wizard of Earthsea*, and even Mickey Mouse has had a chance to play the Inexperienced User of the Black Book. But where did this Black Book come from in the first place? From the Black School, of course!

If you're thinking of applying to the Black School yourself, you'll probably want to know where it's located so you can pack the appropriate clothes. Unfortunately, except for one important exception, the Black School's campus does not appear on any map. The Scandinavians supposed it to be in Wittenberg, Germany, where many of their Lutheran ministers were sent for training, but a few Norwegians placed it in the Spanish university city of Salamanca. According to the Scots, would-be herbalists and magicians went to Italy to study the "Black Airt."

Wherever it might have been on the globe, just about everyone agreed that the Black School was somewhere deep beneath the earth and that its classrooms could only be reached by a ladder or long, downward-sloping passage. There were no windows in the school, no lamps or candlesticks on the desks, for the flaming letters inside the textbooks provided all the light that was needed. There were no doors, since there was no going home or even leaving the building until one's course of study was complete. This could take anywhere from three to seven years, depending on the student's aptitude.

The subterranean setup would have made sense to the

> **Just about everyone agreed that the Black School was somewhere deep beneath the earth and that its classrooms could only be reached by a ladder or long, downward-sloping passage.**

Early Modern Scandinavians whose not-so-distant forebears had sat out on burial mounds whenever they sought the counsel of the ancestral elves who dwelt within them. In the Icelandic version of the Black School, meals were served by a furry gray hand reaching through the wall. The same hand cleared away the dirty dishes and presumably also did the washing up. It was generally understood that this hand belonged to the Devil, but it seems more likely that this particular school was run by an Icelandic troll—a pathologically shy breed of goblin that speaks little, if at all, and often shows no more of himself than a hand or a foot.

Iceland offers us one of the most fully developed Black School traditions, perhaps because the Icelanders had more need of such an institution than their better-connected cousins on the continent. Many of the noblemen in the Norse sagas had sent their children, both male and female, to Finmark to learn the magic arts from the Sami, or "Laplanders." As late as 1920, the folk of Hedmark in eastern Norway were undecided as to whether the eighteenth-century minister Peder Dohn had gained his knowledge of the occult at the school in Wittenberg or up near the Arctic Circle.

As a man of the cloth, Peder Dohn represents the typical Black School graduate. Though neither Satan nor that enterprising Icelandic troll had intended it as such, many students used the Black School as a kind of defense against the dark arts program, eventually turning against the headmaster. Picking a Black School alumnus out of a crowd is not as easy as you'd think. Never mind the guy with the peaked hat, gray beard, and staff; that's just some fellow on his way to the Renaissance Faire. A master of the Black Arts will be much more ordinary in appearance. If he has left the school very recently, he will be marked by a troglodytic pallor. He may be wearing mismatched socks, but, most importantly, he will cast no shadow.

The Black School, as a storytelling tradition, dates only to the beginning of the Protestant era, but many of those who were said to have attended lived much earlier. The school's only required reading, the Black Book, is sometimes referred to as *Cyprianus*, after the most ancient alumnus of all, St. Cyprian of Carthage. Before God made him good, so the story goes, this early church father had studied magic and penned his own tome of helpful spells. Some claim the saint matriculated to the Black School unwittingly, then set down the lessons he learned so that other churchmen might use them in the ongoing battle against Satan. Since then, there have appeared so many versions of this Cyprianus—or Black Book (*Svarte Boken*)—that you should not be surprised if someday you stumble upon a crumbling copy in your favorite used bookshop. To ensure you've bought the real thing, try leaving it on a train, burning it, or tearing out the pages one by one and flushing them down the toilet. If it's the genuine article, it can be neither burned nor drowned nor left behind, which is why you'll never hear the words, "Has anybody seen my Black Book?"

In Scotland, ambitious graduates of the Black School became healers, astrologers, and necromancers, like the famous Renaissance-man-before-his-time Michael Scott (1175–1234). In England, they often found positions as the headmasters of ordinary grammar schools. The latter were a forgetful bunch, often leaving their copies of the Black Book spread open on their blotters, where they invariably attracted the gaze of curious schoolboys. In Scandinavia, as a rule, returned scholars became ministers, while in Central Europe they were more likely to open Black Schools of their own.

One thing all these men had in common was their willingness to accept a challenge. They did not shrink in the face of certain doom, and they never passed the buck. On graduation day, the most accomplished student in the class would volunteer to be the last to file

out the door, not so he could turn out the lights (remember, there weren't any) but so that he could be the one to outwit the Devil. Tuition, you see, was not due until the end of the school year, at which time the Devil claimed the last student to leave. He didn't care who it was as long as he managed to grab *someone* at the end of term.

When Michael Scott reached the end of the passage, and that terrible hand reached out to haul him back, the clever Scott called over his shoulder, "Deel tack the hinmost!"—the hindmost being Scott's own shadow. When Norwegian Peder Dohn dashed up the ladder and out of the school five hundred years later, he used the same trick, promising the Devil that he could keep the shadow so long as Peder never put on two stockings of the same color. From that day forward, Reverend Dohn never left the house in matching stockings, and, of course, he was without a shadow for the rest of his life.

Reports vary as to whether Icelander Saemund the Wise (fl. 1100) gave up his shadow or only his cloak, which he had loosely draped over his shoulders as he sauntered out of the Black School. Either way, it was not the end of it for Saemund, for this time the Devil could

not be fooled so easily. Once Saemund had broken out of the school, he had to perpetrate a series of magical ruses, as a friend had advised him to do in a dream. On his first night of freedom, Saemund carried a blood-filled shoe on his head in order to create a bloody halo around his own personal star in the heavens. Saemund knew that when the Devil realized there was no one inside the cloak, he would seek his whereabouts by scanning the night sky. The red aura around Saemund's star suggested to the Devil that his erstwhile pupil had suffered a violent death. Just to be on the safe side, Saemund carried a shoe filled with brine the next day, so the Devil would think he had drowned, and bloody earth the day after that, so it would appear he was dead and buried.

The most famous Black School graduate you've probably never heard of is Johann von Schadowitz (1624–1704), more commonly known as "Krabat," a nickname given to Croatian soldiers fighting in the army of Elector Johann Georg III. In life, Schadowitz attained fame and glory fighting the Turks. In posthumous legend, Krabat became a powerful sorcerer who had learned his craft at the Black School. As the latter, he is the creation of the Lusatian Sorbs, a Slavic-speaking minority of eastern Germany. In the twentieth century, this folkloric Krabat became known outside the region through a trilogy of books by Sorbian novelist Jurij Brezan and as the titular hero of Otfried Preussler's German language children's novel. Krabat was originally translated into English as *The Satanic Mill*, because that is where the action takes place. Specifically, it is the Black Mill in the village of Schwarzkollm, a place you can indeed find on a map.

While ML 3000 makes much of the escape from the Black School, *Krabat* illustrates what happens inside this half-timbered *Schwarze Schule*, which happens to be a working mill. Preussler's Master of the Black School, a former military man, bears a stronger resemblance to the real Schadowitz than does the novel's hero, the beggar boy turned magical apprentice, Krabat. Here, the Master is not the Devil himself but must take occasional orders from him. He makes reference to other Black Schools, suggesting that he is running the one in Schwarzkollm as a franchise. He's managed to hold on to the mill for a few hundred years already, but he knows that someday one of his apprentices will outstrip him in both talent and wits. That one will either take the Master's place or wash his hands of the dark arts and close the doors of the Black School forever.

Can the Black School ever really be shut down? There might be a last student out the door, but when it comes to the storytelling tradition of ML 3000, there's no last word. So if you're feeling gloomy about living in what sometimes seems

So if you're feeling gloomy about living in what sometimes seems a distinctly non-magical world, rest assured that somewhere in it another writer is even now tapping out the first words of the next chapter in the annals of the Black School.

a distinctly non-magical world, rest assured that somewhere in it another writer is even now tapping out the first words of the next chapter in the annals of the Black School.

Bibliography

Arnason, Jon. *Icelandic Legends*. Translated by Eirikr Magnusson and George E. J. Powell. London: Richard Bentley, 1864. Digitized by Google June 20, 2006.

Christiansen, Reidar. *Folktales of Norway*. Translated by Pat Shaw Iverson. Chicago: The University of Chicago Press, 1964.

Erbrich, Guido, et al. *Wo Krabat das Zaubern lernte*. Bautzen, Germany: Domowina-Verlag, 2010.

Gregor, Walter. *Notes on the Folk-lore of the North-East of Scotland*. Published for the Folklore Society of Great Britain by E. Stock, 1881. Digitized by Google June 20, 2006.

"Die KRABAT-Muehle in Schwarzkollm," http://www.krabatregion.de.

Kvidelund, Reimund, and Henning K. Sehmsdorf, eds. *Scandinavian Folk Belief and Legend*. Minneapolis, MN: University of Minnesota Press, 1988.

Preussler, Otfried. *The Satanic Mill*. Translated by Anthea Bell. Gloucester, MA: Peter Smith, 1985.

Linda Raedisch *is the author of* Night of the Witches: Folklore, Traditions and Recipes for Celebrating Walpurgis Night (*Llewellyn, 2011*). *She lives in northern New Jersey in an apartment crowded with folklore, fairytales, and fantasy novels. She travels often to visit relatives in Germany, returning always with a suitcase full of books. Her next book for Llewellyn,* The Old Magic of Christmas: Yuletide Traditions for the Darkest Days of the Year, *will appear in the fall of 2013.*

Illustrator: Jennifer Hewitson

Columbia:
American Goddess

Mickie Mueller

While planting our vegetable garden, my husband and I got to talking about the concept of a victory garden, and I thought it would be cool to have old "Victory Garden" signs to put in the garden. I starting looking on the Internet for vintage images to inspire me and found all of these beautiful goddess-looking ladies draped in red, white, and blue casting seeds to the earth or holding the bounty of the harvest. I commented to my husband about the beautiful images. He, being a huge history buff, just stated in a matter-of-fact manner, "Oh yes, that's Columbia, the Goddess of America."

"What? We have a goddess? How am I not aware of this?" I stammered.

And he began to tell me about how the founders of this country created a goddess to represent the spirit of our country. I was delighted. "Christian nation, my foot!" or something to that effect was my cheery response. I immediately went into research mode. I had to learn more about this goddess. I could actually feel her looking over my shoulder, smiling, this seemingly long-forgotten goddess ready to breathe new life and become rediscovered. I can't think of a time in our nation's history when we needed her more than now.

Birth of a Goddess

The concept of a goddess as a national patroness was nothing new even in the early days of America. After all, many of the people who founded this country had come here from Great Britain, where

Britannia is their goddess. The founders of the country brought in much of their inspiration for government from the ideals of the Roman Republic, where naturally goddesses were revered.

The name Columbia as an allegory for America was first introduced in the late eighteenth century when the American colonists began to form their own identity and a feeling of general fellowship. The name Columbia had first been introduced in *The Gentlemen's Magazine* in Britain nearly a decade before in their thinly veiled satirical versions of Parliamentary debates over the colonies,

Columbia obviously derived from the name Columbus and clearly representing America. The name was claimed by the colonists and turned around from the original derogatory use in that publication and applied to the figure of a noble goddess of the land, liberty, and freedom. Long before Uncle Sam came along in his suit as a representation of our government, we had Columbia in flowing robes, who came to represent the land, the people, and the ideals of a nation.

Columbia became a very popular poetic representation of American patriotism. In 1776 she was first honored as a true goddess in a beautiful and moving poem, "To His Excellency George Washington," by Phillis Wheatley, where she described Columbia:

> *The goddess comes, she moves divinely fair,*
> *Olive and laurel bind her golden hair:*
> *Wherever shines this native of the skies,*
> *Unnumber'd charms and recent graces rise.*

Wheatley herself was a slave, and her poetry sang the praises of Goddess Columbia, whom she had petitioned to inspire George Washington to lead her country to freedom from oppression. One of Columbia's first lessons is about hope for the future. She is a symbol of the ideals that America strives toward, even if they're ideals yet to be achieved. She reminds us to keep on striving, improving, and looking to the future, knowing that through our good work, the future will be brighter.

A Patriotic Goddess Movement

As a secular goddess figure, Columbia has been through many changes over the years, as have the people of her land. Sometimes she is seen in her form as a Native American princess, with a bow and arrow and eagle feathers in her hair. She is a noble maiden goddess of beginnings and the awakening of something brand-new. In later images, we see her as a Greco/Roman-styled goddess, with robes flowing, sometimes winged, and carrying a shield and spear or pole with a liberty cap on it, or sometimes the liberty cap is worn by the goddess herself. The liberty cap is a brimless soft-cloth cap and comes from the ancient world as a symbol of emancipation from slavery and a celebration of freedom. This is Columbia the protectress of rights, freedom fighter, and goddess of compassion. Sometimes we see the Native American and Greco-Roman aspects of Columbia side by side, and sometimes Columbia is represented as if aspects of both the Native American and Greco/Roman goddesses are morphed into one figure, tying in the past with the future.

In later images, Columbia is sometimes seen wearing a war helmet in the style of the Roman Minerva, who was no doubt an inspiration for her birth. She can also be seen bearing a sword and with a strong expression that tells us she can be a goddess of battle and defense and is not afraid to fight when needed; but, reflecting Minerva, she is often seen holding a book, thus tempering her sword with wisdom. She ended up on posters supporting the suffrage movement to win the vote for women, and she was seen in moving illustrations asking Americans to grow gardens to help with the war effort and strengthen our country from the ground up. Columbia has been represented wearing a wreath of laurel or carrying a wreath of olive leaves, reminding us of the accomplishments of peace and of civic duty to the people. Finally, as one of her other aspects, she holds above a torch, echoing the torch of the mighty Hecate, guiding the way with her light and showing compassion to those in need while watching over America's crossroads.

The name of the capital of America and the seat of government, Washington, DC (District of Columbia), is named for Columbia,

We can summon Columbia as we remember the ideals of wisdom, bravery, strength, and compassion that can bring out the best in America.

much like Athens was named for the Greek goddess Athena. She appeared on many coins and can be seen all over Washington, DC, if you look for her, even on top of the capitol building as Lady Freedom. She once had a very prominent presence as a grand statue right behind the desk of the Speaker of the House in the House of Representatives. Seen as Columbia Liberty, she was flanked by her totem animals, the eagle and the snake, and watched over our elected officials. The grand statue was moved to the National Statuary Hall in 1857, unfortunately, for I personally feel that her presence is needed to help guide and heal the United States. Also bearing her name are Columbia University, numerous ships, and even a space shuttle. She's the woman you see at the beginning of all Columbia Pictures films, torch held high. The original unofficial national anthem was "Hail Columbia" and is now the song played for the entrance of the Vice President.

Columbia is literally everywhere and yet somehow has been forgotten after all these years. We as Pagans and Witches can reclaim her power as we shape our futures the way so many have before us. We can summon Columbia as we remember the ideals of wisdom, bravery, strength, and compassion that can bring out the best in America. Call upon her to banish the fear, prejudices, and greed that can only hold America back. Columbia is not so much a symbol of what we are now as a nation as what we want to be in the future— embracing freedom, liberty, and justice in new ways.

Magical Correspondences for Goddess Columbia

The following is a list of magical correspondences that can be used in spellwork to honor Columbia and to petition her assistance. These can be added to spellwork or placed on your altar when working with her. Human rights, religious freedom, protecting the sacred land—these are all duties that Columbia would be happy to take on as a patron goddess, if only we would ask.

Symbols: Liberty cap and pole, shield, eagle feathers, sword, bow and arrow, torch, war helmet, sun-ray crown, five-pointed stars, broken chains

Animals: Eagle, rattlesnake, dove

Plants: Olive, laurel, pears, apples

Colors: Red, blue, white, gold, purple

Celestial bodies: Venus, Sun

Zodiac: The constellation Virgo

Powers/Attributes: Liberty and freedom, freedom from slavery, war, agriculture and abundance, hope, prosperity, striving to reach ideals, honor, perseverance, strength in battle, civic duty, care for the poor, overcoming tyranny, women's rights, protection of soldiers, community, fair trade and commerce

Victory Garden Blessing

Columbia blesses the land with abundance, and she is happy to help those who help themselves. During the World Wars, the people were encouraged to grow Victory Gardens. By growing their own vegetables, fruits, and herbs, the people had a way to supplement the public food supplies. Today, growing a Victory Garden means growing food

to help us become victorious over a challenging economy. There is no better goddess to bless your Victory Garden than Columbia.

Mix 1 cup of milk with 1 tablespoon of honey poured into a shallow dish. You'll also need a wooden spoon or a small sprig from either an apple or a pear tree. Before you plant your seeds, use the spoon or sprig to dip into the honey milk and shake it over your garden, asperging it with the blessings of abundance. As you do, repeat the following charm:

Columbia, bless this fertile soil
Within it I will plant and toil
As I sow the seeds of victory
And grow my family prosperity.

You may also wish to hang ribbons in Columbia's colors from tomato cages, decorate with a vintage Victory Garden sign of Columbia, or draw her symbols on the backs of your garden markers.

. . . .

Columbia carries with her the spirit of history and hope for the future, along with the energy of all people who have overcome the odds. Witches of America, let's bring the magic of this goddess back to life for the greater good.

BIBLIOGRAPHY

Hoyt, Albert H. *The Name "Columbia."* Boston, MA: D. Clapp & Son, 1886.

Pencak, William, Matthew Dennis, and Simon P. Newman, eds. *Riot and Revelry in Early America.* University Park: Pennsylvania State University Press, 2002.

Wheatley, Phillis. *Complete Writings.* Edited by Vincent Carretta. New York: Penguin Books, 2001.

Mickie Mueller *is an award-winning and critically acclaimed artist of fantasy, fairy, and myth. She is an ordained Pagan minister and has studied Natural Magic, Fairy Magic, and Celtic tradition. She is also a Reiki master/teacher in the Usui Shiki Ryoho tradition. She enjoys creating magical art full of fairies, goddesses, and beings of folklore. She works primarily in a mix of colored pencil and watercolor infused with magical herbs corresponding to her subject matter. Mickie is the illustrator of* The Well Worn Path *and* The Hidden Path *decks, the writer/illustrator of* Voice of the Trees: A Celtic Divination Oracle, *and the illustrator of the* Mystical Cats Tarot, *coming in 2014. Mickie is a regular contributor to several of the Llewellyn annuals.*

Illustrator: Tim Foley

From Dominance to Guardianship: Gaia's Great Permaculture Movement

Estha McNevin

The first time I heard about the ecological design principles of permaculture, our temple was hosting an
outrageously fun and semi-nomadic
Pagan family of Earth activists: the Wilsons. In more ways than one, their off-
the-grid lifestyle helped our Thelemic,
Neopagan temple to learn the funda-
mentals of integrated organic farming and economic sustainability. They
reacquainted us with the Appalachian
survival manuals the *Foxfire* series, introduced us to Starhawk's spiritual work
with permaculture, and shared insights
from Toby Hemenway's *Gaia's Garden:
A Guide to Home-Scale Permaculture*. By

passing on work that had served as a foundation for their own quest for sustainability, they inspired our whole coven to chuck the city and go country. Using integrated ecological design models that mimic Mother Nature's own diverse and abundant ecosystems has continued to offer our small farm new ways to lower our impact on the environment while improving our own health and the organic quality of the foods we cultivate for our growing community.

Our friendship with Delyla, Stan, and their daughter, Megan, motivated our spiritual redirection toward primitive skills, group cooperation, and fair labor distribution. From our raised-bed gardens, to the chickens and turkeys, to the well-worshiped orchard, the Wilsons have been a consummate source of rural survival information and support. More than anything, they really got us fired up about the permaculture skills movement as a political and ethical path of true Neopagan stability.

Upon further tilling the themes of the movement, I discovered that, like Starhawk, other enlightened academics such as Dr. Elaine Ingham presented lectures and demonstrated techniques for ecological soil building. By cutting out the chemicals and using worms, fungi, local insects, and regionally specific microorganisms, permaculture encourages gardeners toward spiritual and artistic (as well as intelligent and functional) design. A microbiologist and pedology specialist  concerned with soil formation, Dr. Ingham believes that we have to go back to the natural system and really study how nature flourishes. If we truly hope to thrive for generations yet to come, then we have work to do. Her evidence against pesticides converted me to the organic gardening standard—lock, stock, and worm bucket.

Much of Dr. Ingham's work unequivocally demonstrates the microbial perfection of naturally healthy, organic soil. This creates a humus-rich result, in which all manner of fungi, bacteria, and organisms live long and fulfilling lives. As they enrich the ecosystem, they aid in the nitrogen cycle. Nearly all of our fruits and vegetables thrive in this type of soil. When organic soils are compared to chemically dependent ones, the utter lack of microbial life found in enriched alchemical loams really does make any vegetable grown in them seem an unnatural miracle!

Starhawk and Ingham, along with other academics in the sustainability movement, profess the unbroken perfection of the earth's own natural ecosystem as a sacred web or spiritual network of life. Many frontrunners in the movement set a new model for Pagan ethics by holding themselves intellectually and spiritually accountable for the state of our planet. If, like our own Pagan ancestors, we believe Gaia Sophia to be a true sentient life force, then surely our worship and adoration of her should include the exacting study of her design. Permaculture really made me aware of the Pagan need for self-sustainability. To adore the earth in ritual and song, and then choose not to compost or recycle, is to worship a dying goddess—not one seeing a revival.

The original permaculture concept was co-founded by Australian naturalist Bill Mollison and Tasmanian ecologist David Holmgren during the late 1970s, while both men were serving as faculty for the University of Tasmania. Their aim was to help lessen the impact that human development has on the planet. As a result of their work, many organic agricultural engineers now use a more credibly productive cultivation model, attempting to unite humanity and nature by emulating wild-land models of verdant agronomy.

The fundamental ethics of sustainability charge every human being with the power to take care of Earth, to take care of the people, and finally, to share the surplus.

One of the things I love the most about permaculture is that it uses a more ancient sense of guardianship to engender social, civic, and environmental accountability. The fundamental ethics of sustainability charge every human being with the power to take care of Earth, to take care of the people, and finally, to share the surplus. Imagine for a moment if our global stockpiles of oil, sugar, rice, and corn were used more to feed the poor than they were to pad agricultural subsidies and the federal stock exchange. What would our world even look like if our economy were truly sustainable instead of inflated by debt?

. . . .

So much of our developing world is still evolving toward fair and healthy labor standards. If each and every person on the planet was guaranteed civil and human rights, the prices on the shelf would look startlingly different. Like many other global spiritualists, I can't help but think of the ol' Wiccan Rede or the Hindu principle of woven karma; after all, aren't we supposed to live by the model "fairly take and fairly give"? Permaculture works because it is a movement founded on greater notions of social and environmental responsibility. This is perhaps the greatest reason why locavores stress a "keep it local" philosophy, which must legitimately support the community, the grocer, the distributor, the farmer, the family, and the self.

Where we get our food matters. Choosing to keep our money in the local economy gives smaller farmers and ranchers a chance against corporate GMO giants like Monsanto. Engaging in locavorism means supporting our regional food producers by shopping at co-ops and farmers' markets, eating seasonally, and consuming in terms of one's surrounding environment. Keeping it local also means committing to the most effective model of community sustainability through daily personal choice.

· · · · · · · · · · · · ·

The modern Wiccan and Neopagan movements have always been interwoven with civil rights and environmentalism because of our old-world values toward nature as a living divine being, of which we are but a single part. Our love and Gnostic adoration of Gaia Sophia has been a constant catalyst for the evolution of Western agriculture. Through our mythic and shamanic systems, humanity has kept a genuine sense of "Mother Earth" alive in the many ways that we celebrate her seasonal cycles. How we worship the earth is ever changing alongside Gaia Sophia herself.

To me, permaculture is that next step in our revival of such old ways—not so that we might regress into agricultural serfdom, but instead to ensure that we evolve our animistic spirituality further as we work to truly live in perfect harmony with the goddess of all things living. To do this, we must choose to aspire to a more complete understanding of our personal impact on the ecosystem in which we live. If our families and communities are to thrive, we will have to adapt our choices to match our spiritual and naturalistic ethics seamlessly, which brings into question everything from our plastic Isis sculptures to the energetic and karmic purity of the foods we eat.

Ethically produced agriculture requires a fair trade–based sustainable cycle for humans, animals, vegetables, and minerals alike. We all know that fair is not always cheap, and one of the enlightening things about permaculture is that it utilizes biomimicry to transform the mistakes of our past into the paradise of our future. Moreover, if we solve our environmental problems with permaculture, we must come to terms with the moral and economic divide in our own Pagan culture. The nearer we live to the natural cycles of the earth, the closer we are to the Goddess.

Many coven structures out there continue to carry on idealizing a feudal cast model as if it were a sacred path of enlightenment by divine selection rather than natural selection. The little people toil while the enlightened Lords and Ladies hold the keys. However, in the West we have evolved to view similar ancient caste models as a violation of basic human rights when they still occur in parts of Asia, India, and the Middle East. Our own evolution towards sustainable communities may depend more on labor equality than we prefer to recognize in Paganism. After all, so many of our rituals are still designed around the social and political models of younger, less evolved Victorian cultures, many of which were merely attempting to emulate the aesthetics of our ancient Pagan civilizations. Our Wiccan and occult forefathers were not trying to revive the total religious infrastructure of antiquity. Even if the old ones did enjoy the glory of their own age, few of us are keen to reintroduce their outdated caste practices, like forced marriage, abject slavery, and aristocratic theology. The future of Paganism as a whole demands our constant change and expansive diversity. Permaculture and locavorism are the best chances we have of enriching and evolving our own ancient Pagan cultures toward a truly sustainable and self-governing capacity to maintain our own culture.

Dominion over Gaia Sophia is still the singular goal of industrial manufacturers, mining firms, and natural resource giants. For generations, our banking systems have used our greatest fears and insecurities against us. Those in positions of power have purchased our silence and loyalty with cheaper, easier, and better pollutants, many of which are still in our homes, cars, and public spaces, where they poison us as well as our planet. Permaculture offers a different solution: an organically engineered future that is fair, abundant, and sustainable because we choose to make it so. For many Pagans, viable agriculture is a form of karmic accountability. With our feet firmly planted in the soil, we do feel closer to our roots.

This year, as our local economies shoulder the reality of global warming and the world market, it is the interconnectedness and shared empathy of our own diverse Pagan cultures that can help to further the global cooperative permaculture movement. As spiritually aware families across the planet seek new ways to live abundant and sustainable lives, we will all have to reevaluate the integrity of our daily choices and learn new ways to embrace the innovations destined to ensure our own cultural survival. Far up in the hills here

in Montana, our farm and orchard are banking on the biological diversity of the permaculture model to heal and enrich Gaia Sophia for as long as we are lucky enough to have guardianship of her.

RESOURCES

Foxfire, https://www.foxfire.org/magazine.html

Starhawk's Tangled Web, http://www.starhawk.org

Belili Productions, http://www.belili.org/permaculture/Permaculture _GrowingEdge.html

Holmgren Design Services, http://www.holmgren.com.au

Earth Activist Training, http://www.earthactivisttraining.org

The Permaculture Association of Tasmania, http://permaculturetas.org/x/x

Biomimicry 3.8, http://biomimicry.net

Ask Nature, http://www.asknature.org

Estha McNevin (*Missoula, MT*) *is the founding Priestess and oracle of the Eastern Hellenistic magickal temple Opus Aima Obscuræ (OAO). As High Priestess of OAO, she teaches concise Pagan history, metaphysical skills, ritual practicum, and art. In the greater community she works as a lecturer, baker, writer, organic gardener, and psychic intuitive and is co-owner of the metaphysical business Twigs & Brews. In addition to hosting public rituals for the sabbats, Estha organizes coven holiday events and women's divination rituals each Dark Moon. She conducts private spiritual consultations, spirit intermediations, and Tarot readings for the greater Pagan community. Visit her at www.facebook.com/opusaimaobscurae.*

Illustrator: Bri Hermanson

Witchy Living

DAY-BY-DAY WITCHCRAFT

Using Creative Visualization to Make Your Life More Magical

Barbara Ardinger, PhD

Think of someone in your life who is annoying. Perhaps it's a coworker or a neighbor. Not an evil person who's making you want to get out the reversing candles and do a full-on spell, but just a pest. What, specifically, is this person doing? How does what this person does or says annoy you? How often? Now add this element: this is a person you have to get along with. You have to keep peace in the office or neighborhood.

Visualization to Neutralize a Pesky Person

Close your eyes and take several deep, easy breaths until you're in your alpha state. Your body is relaxed and your mind is alert and active. Bring to mind the Wiccan Rede: *Harm no one.* You don't want to harm this pesky person, just neutralize his or her actions.

Visualize the infinity symbol (∞). Let it be whatever color it wants to be, but if it appears red, purple, or black, then recolor it using pink, green, or maybe light blue. You want it to symbolize peace and friendship, not anger or dominance. Now grow the infinity symbol until it's big enough for a person to stand in. Take another deep, easy breath.

Step into one side of the symbol. Stand there alone for a minute and absorb feelings of friendship, amity, concord, and peace. If you want to, let these feelings manifest as a gentle rain.

Call your coworker or neighbor into the other side of the symbol. Share your feelings of friendship, amity, and concord with him or her. Let the feelings rain down upon that person, and speak frankly but politely and say it's time to put peskiness, jealousy, anger, and discord aside.

Become silent and let the gentle rain of amity and concord continue to touch you and the other person until you feel you've soaked up as much as you can. When it's time—and you'll know when it's time—open gates in both sides of the infinity symbol. Walk out. You and the other person can go your separate ways, but know that when you meet again, it will be a friendly meeting.

Take several more deep, easy breaths, and open your eyes and come back to our world of consensual reality. Do this visualization at dawn or at sunset for nine days in a row, preferably when the moon is waxing.

The Power of Visualization

As Pagans, we know that visualization works. It's probably a safe bet that every one of us has been led through a guided visualization at a workshop or ritual. Most often, we're led into a wilderness, along a beach, or down a flight of ancient steps. We walk into the woods or into a cave and meet a divine being who gives us a teaching and then sends us home again. Sometimes these visualizations change our lives.

Understanding that it's wrong to manipulate people against their will (like make them fall in love with us) or to do harm, we work in many ways. We're doing magic, of course, and we also know that "as above, so below" also means "as inside, so outside."

It's handy to remember that we don't always have to do elaborate visualizations to get good, useful results. It's not necessary to cast a circle every time, or to light candles (though it's nice) or chant or drum. When we turn to smaller visualizations, like the one opening this article, we can be sitting in our cubicle apparently studying our computer screen or a corporate report. We can be standing on the front porch or on the sidewalk. Just please, don't do a visualization while you're driving. It's bad enough that people text or play with the screens in the dashboards of their fancy new cars while they're driving. We've all been on busy streets or freeways behind a car zig-zagging across lanes or going in fits and starts. Don't be a dangerous driver. Do your visualization where you're grounded, *not on wheels*.

Brief visualizations almost always come in handy. Sometimes you have to use stronger magic and need a more powerful symbol than a neutral infinity sign. Back in the days when I was a technical writer, I had to work with an engineer on the fourth floor of the building. Don't get me wrong—I always enjoyed working with the engineers. I would read what one of the guys wrote about a weapons system or cement or software, blink my eyes several times, then pat

him on the knee and say, "Just let me turn this into gooder English for you." It worked every time. Except with the guy on the fourth floor. His work was perfect. It never needed to be edited. (Wanna bet?) And besides that, he kept coming on to me. He had creeping (and creepy) hands. The infinity symbol didn't even begin to work with him. So I got out the magical envelope.

Visualization to Neutralize an Extremely Annoying Person

Think of an extremely annoying person, someone you really need to get away from. As mainstream metaphysicians teach us, everyone has their own perfect place, and that place is not necessarily where we are.

Find someplace where you won't be interrupted. Sit comfortably and take several deep, easy breaths. Close your eyes and enter your alpha state.

Summon the magical envelope. The envelope is large. It's usually padded, and it seems to have wings. Also conjure up a roll of duct tape. You may need it. As you watch the envelope and duct tape fly toward you, state your intention: "I want to send this person to his or her proper place. Let him or her go unharmed, but let him or her

go away from me. And never come back!"

What color is the envelope? If it's an angry color at first (such as red, purple, or black), that's okay. Ditto for the duct tape.

Now summon the person who is making you so angry or afraid. As this person comes

closer, he or she gets smaller and the envelope gets bigger. Help the person crawl into the envelope. Know that you're not injuring this person. There's plenty of oxygen in there, and the envelope is padded. Close the envelope and seal it. If the person is obstreperous, you may want to wrap the duct tape around the envelope three or four times. You gotta keep that annoying person inside.

With the envelope completely sealed, hold it in your projective hand (right hand if you're right-handed, left if you're left-handed). If it's still an angry color, ask it to turn to a calmer color. Green and white are good. Say a firm goodbye to the person inside, then throw the envelope over your left shoulder. Let it sail off into outer space. *Do not look where it's going. Do not turn around.* Let it go away. You don't want to know where. Be aware that even if the person doesn't go away physically, he or she will go away from you. The engineer I worked with stayed on the fourth floor for another year, but for some reason I wasn't assigned to work with him anymore, and he somehow never came down to the second floor, at least not while I was there.

Say goodbye to the person again, then take several deep, easy breaths and open your eyes. Go back to work and do whatever needs to be done in your physical reality.

Note: As I write this, family members of a friend are trying to intimidate me. I've put them in a box that looks like the one in which the aviator put the Little Prince's sheep in the Saint-Exupéry book. It's closed with duct tape. Five days. So far, so good.

Healing with Visualization

The symbols we use in magic and visualization are important. Most Pagans know what the colors mean (if you don't, find a good list of the chakra correspondences) and how to use symbols of the elemental powers. For the brief visualizations described here, the homey, everyday symbols are most effective. They're the easiest to see clearly (we probably see envelopes every day), and we can hold them in our minds more easily. Be aware that while a symbol like an envelope is simple, it's not weak. After all, we can pick up a pencil and use it as a wand instead of a willow withe as thick as our thumb and as long as our arm from elbow to finger. It's the power we project into our symbols and tools that makes them powerful, at least on a personal level. It's also more entertaining—and our minds do like to be entertained—to use a symbol that's not on the list of proper symbols we found in some book. Make up your own symbols when you do brief visualizations. Because they're personal, they'll bring more magic into your life as you use them.

Make up your own symbols when you do brief visualizations. Because they're personal, they'll bring more magic into your life as you use them.

Witches, medicine men and women, shamans, and other Pagans have traditionally been healers. We can also heal ourselves. When I had a very annoying cancer in 2003, I went at it on many levels. I went to a terrific surgeon named Dr. Mimi, and after the surgery I got a lot of CT scans, plus a PET scan. A good friend did a Reiki treatment on me. I was placed in the center of at least three magical circles and bombarded with healing rays. And every morning and every evening, I used Goddess Goo.

Goddess Goo? It's imaginary. I visualized it. Goddess Goo comes in a tube or jar, it's the consistency it needs to be (from watery to almost abrasive), and it's the color it needs to be. Before my surgery, at dawn and dusk, I rubbed Goddess Goo on the site of the cancer, both inside my body and outside. At that time, the Goddess Goo was mostly grass green. After the surgery, I kept using it, and it turned blue. One time it was so watery that it flowed through the veins and arteries throughout my body. I didn't require radiation or chemotherapy, and after three years they told me I'd had enough CT scans. My health is good, and the scar is barely visible. I've recommended Goddess Goo—and explained what it is and how to imagine and use it—to people with skin cancers, to a friend who was having hip replacement surgery, and to people I don't even remember anymore. You can use it, too.

Visualization to Heal Yourself with Goddess Goo

This visualization is best done lying in bed. Close your eyes, take several deep, easy breaths, and enter your alpha state. In visualization, we can be as big or as small as we want to be, and we can go wherever we want to go. With the eyes of your imagination, see yourself as tiny enough to stand inside your physical body.

Suddenly you're holding something in your hand. Look at what you're holding. Perhaps it's a big jar that looks like cold cream. Perhaps it's a big tube that looks like sunscreen. The label says "Goddess Goo. Good For What Hurts." Scoop or squeeze a bit out. What is its consistency? What color is it? What does it smell like? Set the jar or tube down and rub the goo in your hands. What does it feel like?

Pick up your jar or tube and walk to the place in your body that needs to be treated. Massage the Goddess Goo into that spot. Massage some more goo around the area. Go outside your body and massage some goo into your skin above the site. Does it tingle? Become warm or cool? Is there a smell?

You have a never-ending supply of Goddess Goo. Rub the Goddess Goo where it hurts—before or after surgery, after athletic injuries, on sprains and breaks—at dawn and dusk every day until you're healed. *Also be sure to get proper medical treatment. Goddess Goo is not a substitute for proper medical treatment.*

Making Plans and Decisions with Visualization

It often happens that we need to make an important decision. It's time to stop procrastinating, time to solve that knotty problem or do some forward planning. But we just can't get it together. Maybe we have too many options, or too few and none of them are good. We can't focus, so we sit at our desk or on the couch and send texts or play games when we should be doing some serious thinking. Spend the money for that nifty new technological device? Go to graduate school? Where? Take out a loan? Let ourselves be vulnerable and get closer to a potentially special him or her? Get over him or her? Get over it in general? Take a stand on some important political or social issue? Get out of some closet or other? If we want to truly live our lives, we need to make decisions and plans. We can use creative visualization to help ourselves.

Visualization to Make a Decision

First calm down and stop worrying. Take several deep, easy breaths, close your eyes, and enter your alpha state. In meditation and visualization, we can of course be both the observer and the one who is observed. See yourself as you probably appear to others right now. You're just sitting there, doing nothing. You've turned into an unconscious, unthinking vegetable. What kind of vegetable? Does that symbol tell you anything about yourself?

What you need is a thinking cap. Create or summon a thinking cap. What does it look like? Is it a tall, conical wizard's hat to help you with your magic? A scholarly skullcap? A nice academic mortarboard with a gold tassel? A sophisticated beret? A leather aviator's helmet? A Panama hat? Indiana Jones's fedora? Mickey Mouse ears? Select the perfect thinking cap for your situation. (Try not to be sarcastic.)

Hand the thinking cap to the mini-you that you're observing. Place it on your head. Your specialized thinking cap has special powers. Feel those powers brushing your hair, soaking into your scalp, and flowing into the appropriate parts of your brain. You're already beginning to think of ways to solve your problem.

Now visualize the old cliché, the light bulb above the head. Reach out and turn on the light. See light radiating in all directions, with special beams illuminating your thinking cap and strengthening the cap's special cognitive powers. Is your hair glowing? The light bulb, of course, symbolizes direct inspiration. It's insight. Illumination. Enlightenment.

You can make your decision! See your mini-you smile and nod. See yourself pick up a pencil and start writing. See yourself turn to your keyboard and start typing. See yourself doing necessary research and making lists.

If necessary, keep the thinking cap on your head and do this visualization at dawn and sunset every day for nine days.

. . . .

Just as we can learn to heal ourselves, we can also teach ourselves things we don't even know we know. You can also create your own thinking cap. In another visualization, go into that famous cave or into those famous woods, put on your thinking cap, and have a conversation with the divine being you meet. Know that you will remember what you learned when you come back to consensual reality. If you don't remember right away, be patient. Messages can come, as we know, in surprising ways.

. . . .

Use creative visualization to build stronger magic in your life. As long as you remember the Wiccan Rede, *Harm none*, your visualizations will make life better for you and those around you. See what I mean?

Barbara Ardinger, PhD (*www.barbaraardinger.com*), *is the author of* Secret Lives, *a novel about a circle of crones, mothers, and maidens, plus goddesses, a talking cat, and the Green Man. Her earlier books include* Pagan Every Day, Goddess Meditations, Finding New Goddesses (*a parody of goddess encyclopedias*), *and* Quicksilver Moon (*a realistic novel … except for the vampire*). *Her day job is freelance editing for people who have good ideas but don't want to embarrass themselves in print. To date, she has edited more than 250 books, both fiction and nonfiction, on a wide range of topics. Barbara lives in Southern California with her two rescued Maine coon cats, Heisenberg and Schroedinger.*

Illustrator: Christa Marquez

Touched by the Spirit World

Emyme

I put aside the book, took off my glasses, turned off the light, and settled down to sleep for the night. As I slipped into a doze, the cat jumped on the bed and curled up near my feet. The first time it happened I was startled completely awake. I had to look, to be sure. I had to be sure there was nothing there—because there was no cat. Sadly, our Sassycat had passed.

Another living cat strolled through the room, stopped, and suddenly took off running into the hall. Near the coat rack she jumped as high as she could and batted at the wall. Repeatedly. Finally giving up, she stretched out on her

back next to the baseboard, stared in the general direction of the ceiling for a while, then got up and went about her day.

A time of upheaval in my life had me under quite a bit of stress on several fronts. One day at work, while wallowing in sadness and self-pity, I felt a comforting hand at the small of my back. Turning, there was no one there, no one even close.

Almost every religion and belief system contains in their dogma the possibility of an invisible spirit world. During my ongoing journey to Earth-based polytheism, I have opened my mind and heart to spirits and welcome their touch in my life with no fear.

Pet Energy Remains in Your Home

Our beloved pets often leave behind a trace after they have passed on. You settle on the couch for a nap, relax in your favorite chair to read, or turn in for the night, and after a few minutes your cat or dog jumps up to join you as always—but they have been gone for days, weeks, or even several years. You hear your bird sing, or the squeak of the hamster wheel, and the cage is long since empty and packed away. You may even hear the hum of the water filter even though you dismantled the fish tank ages ago.

Always greet them—speak out loud or offer a silent hello. Leave space for them; do not crowd out their former resting spot. Do not immediately change the environment or pack up their belongings: bed, blanket, cage, tank, toys. If you have other pets and/or if you get new pets, explain to them in very simple terms that a spirit may still be in the home and there is nothing to fear. If there had been a special bond between the deceased pet and another pet, expect some mourning. Animals are blessed and innocent, as are children. Do not be surprised or alarmed if children recognize the energy of a pet no longer in residence.

Remain open-minded, openhearted, and welcoming. Remember all the special times spent with your companion. Never fear.

Otherworldly Beings Share Your Surroundings

Fairies, pixies, brownies, sprites, or elves; salamanders, undines, gnomes, and sylphs—I must admit from the outset that I have no tangible, definitive proof of contact with these creatures. However, I fervently believe there are numerous forms of spiritual energy on the earth that we are not, or rarely, meant to see. Perhaps you share these experiences with me:

- While gardening in the heat of the day with no breeze, you feel an unexpected gust of wind. Leaves float down. The sylphs are playing.

- What made that little valley in the mulch—a chipmunk or a squirrel? The gnomes are reasserting their age-old hold on a little bit of Earth.

- See those ripples in the birdbath? With no bug or bird around to disturb the surface? The undines are enjoying a refreshing splash.

- Staring into the flame of a candle or a fire, feel the salamanders hypnotize and calm.

- What is that insect never seen before, the one that just popped up out of nowhere? Is that a fairy or wood sprite in disguise?

Tiny rainbows, the sound of music or laughter, an unfamiliar scent, small items moved in your home or yard—each and every one of these is a sure sign of being blessed by unseen energies. Look beyond the obvious in the yard and garden, in blowing leaves and seeds, in the birdbath, in candle-flame. If you are so inclined, create places they may live and rest undisturbed. Offer gifts and refreshments: a small sparkly trinket or pretty scrap of fabric, a bottle cap full of honey or wine. Remain open-minded, open-hearted, and welcoming. Do not doubt. Never fear.

Tiny rainbows, the sound of music or laughter, an unfamiliar scent, small items moved in your home or yard—each and every one of these is a sure sign of being blessed by unseen energies.

Your Spirit Guide/Angel Is Revealed to You

Earlier in my religious journey, the doctrine and the rituals of the Catholic Church called to me. Saints fascinated me. Angels were a popular topic, and I became intrigued by the idea of discovering my personal guardian angel's name. My religious mentor instructed me on the way to determine the name. It is very simple, and I share it here: ask.

That was it, just ask. No matter your belief—angel or spirit guide—this method works. Ask for their name. Ask them to let you know in such a way that you will have no doubt. Ask for a physical/visceral sign when the name is shown to you. Ask to be shown the name in various forms—like a street sign, a billboard, an article in a magazine, or a commercial on television. Ask out loud, or in a silent prayer. Ask on paper, and put the paper away. Do not reject a name because you think, "Well, it cannot possibly be that name. I have never liked that name." Do not be disappointed because you had hoped for your favorite name. On the other hand, do not rush to the name haphazardly. Give it a hard deadline—seriously. Otherwise, after a few weeks of waiting you may be willing to grab at any old name—for example, after the twelfth time you have seen an advertisement for Wendy's fast food. While you are waiting for the answer, concentrate on names that have cropped up over and over in your life. Have you had more than one friendly or romantic relationship with people of the same name? Does a name keep coming at you—more often and varied than just seeing the Wendy's fast food commercial twelve times—perhaps in a song, on billboards, or in overheard conversations?

Armed with this instruction, I asked to be presented with the name of my guardian angel, in an easily recognizable and definite way, within one work week. I asked to receive a physical feeling when I knew I had the right name. Then I waited. I asked on a Sunday, and by Wednesday I was getting frustrated. During lunch break I went to my car and noticed a quarter on the ground at my feet by the driver's door. Out of habit, I picked it up and put it in my pocket, as I do with almost any coin I find in my travels. At a convenience store I saw two more quarters outside the entrance. I picked them up and put them in my pocket.

Driving back to my job, I started to think about those coins. My car had been parked next to a curb; no one could have exited another vehicle and dropped a coin. The coins at the store were in plain sight on the sidewalk. I had seen a person walk right over that very spot. In both cases I had heard no coins drop—quarters are heavy enough to make a distinct sound. So I began to think... quarters...what is it about quarters? What name could come from a quarter? Who is on a quarter? And suddenly there it was, that physical/visceral feeling for which I had asked: a wave of energy passed through me as I realized it was George. The name of my guardian angel was George, which made complete sense to me. My "imaginary" childhood friend was George, and he was big—much bigger than I. Being fond of all things British, St. George is one of my favorite saints. One of my grandfathers was named George. Twenty years and more than a dozen experiences later, I am more certain than ever of George. Be he an angel or a spirit guide, George is my constant companion.

· · · · · · · · · · · · ·

Once you have learned the name of your guardian angel/personal guide, here are a few ways in which they may make their presence known:

- When going through a difficult time, you feel a hand upon your shoulder in comfort.

- You are about to say something in anger to a colleague, friend, or loved one, and feel a hand upon the small of your back as if in warning.

- Out of the corner of your eye, in your peripheral vision, you see movement or a shadow.

- There is a breeze where there can be none, or it is suddenly hot or cold.

- Your name is called as you drift to sleep, or in that dozy/dreamy state before waking.

To the extreme:

- The steering wheel is yanked out of your hands to avoid an accident.

- You are physically pulled back from stepping off a curb or entering a building.

- A trip is delayed due to a lost object, and you miss an accident by minutes—only to find that object in plain sight later.

Remember, this energy is benevolent and beneficial, has a personal interest in you, and is invested in your well-being.

. . . .

No matter your level of education or immersion into Earth-based belief systems, know that spirits exist. Just beyond the veil of our sight is a universe of energy and beings that touch our lives in personal and positive ways. This individual piece of writing is too short to do complete justice to an examination of the topic. It is my wish to have piqued your interest enough for further study. I leave you with this last bit of advice: remain open-minded, openhearted, and welcoming. And never fear.

Emyme, *an eclectic solitary, resides in a multi-generation, multi-cat household in Southern New Jersey—concentrating on candle spells, garden spells, and kitchen witchery. In addition to writing poetry and prose about strong women of mythology and fairy tales, Emyme is creating a series of articles on bed & breakfasts from the point of view of the over-55, single, female, Wiccan traveler. Please send questions or comments to catsmeow24@verizon.net.*

Illustrator: Kathleen Edwards

Magical De-Stressing

Lisa Mc Sherry

You hear it all the time, from almost everyone you know: "I'm so stressed." "I feel overwhelmed." "I can't get caught up." Stress is the defining characteristic of the twenty-first century, and sometimes it seems impossible to manage, which creates more stress— I call it the negative feedback loop of DOOM. When we are stressed, we usually feel helpless and out of control.

Do not despair! There are simple things you can do to break the feedback loop of doom and reduce the stress—or even dissipate it completely.

Relieving Work Worry

I have a career that I love, but it often has a stressful component. Making sure I have touchstones of my faith around me serves a twofold purpose: I have allies to call upon in managing negative situations, and the objects serve as constant reminders that there is more to my life than what takes place at my job.

In most cases, you can have objects that hold personal meaning on your desk or in your cube at work. I have never felt comfortable having anything that resembled an altar in my workspace, but I do have a small statue of Ganesh (clearer of obstacles) and a carved stone bowl full of polished stones. He likes sweets and the color red, so I'll often put a candy bar there, on a small swatch of red fabric. When things get stressful, I give myself a break (even five minutes will do), take a deep breath, center myself, and call upon Ganesh for assistance.

Essential oils are another subtle but effective way to de-stress in the office environment. The oils are intensely concentrated, so a very little bit goes a long way (which helps when spending thirty dollars on a tiny bottle). Essential oils directly affect the olfactory sense, bypassing the neocortex and going directly to the "reptilian brain," the oldest part of our brain and the part that most affects how we perceive and experience danger and stress. Smell can transport us to a different place, breaking a cycle of stress that threatens to overwhelm us.

Essential oils are another subtle but effective way to de-stress in the office environment.... Smell can transport us to a different place, breaking a cycle of stress that threatens to overwhelm us.

Here are my three favorite stress-busting essential oils:

- **Lavender.** Widely available and cheap, even for organically grown high-quality oils, this oil is super-effective for most people, is nearly instantaneous in its effect, and has the lowest allergic reaction rate I have heard of over the years.

- **Lemon.** Floral scents can be overwhelming or off-putting, in which case I recommend lemon (or any citrus scent). The scent is refreshing and is often associated with relaxing summer days. Lemon also produces saliva, counteracting the dry mouth often associated with stress.

- **Eucalyptus.** This is a sharp, clear, menthol scent (peppermint is an alternative if you can't find eucalyptus) that refreshes the mind.

The easiest way to use these scents is to put a few drops on a cotton handkerchief before you leave home and carry it with you in a small Ziploc bag. When you get stressed, open the bag and take three deep breaths with the cloth close to your nose. Take your time with the breaths, allowing them to clear your mind and relax your body.

When I was going through a particularly stressful time several years ago, I wore a locket necklace with a small pad inside, and every morning I refreshed the scent on the pad. The warmth of my skin sent the scent directly into my nose all day long.

Looking at calming images is a great way to sneak de-stressing time into your office routine. Some of my favorites include a live feed of a bunch of puppies and an osprey's nest (see www.explore.org). Swimming fish relaxes many people. Or how about a sunset by the ocean? Each feed is less than ten minutes long, so you'll still have time during your break to get a drink or make a phone call.

Reducing Health Hassles

If you are ill or worried about your health, the stress is doubled by the worry, and it is especially important to de-stress often and to pay attention to steering the mind away from worrying. The body needs all the help it can get to restore itself, and the best thing we can do from our end is to reduce health stress by staying calm and to keep the mind as peaceful as possible.

Essential oils are useful with this as well. I like parsley, sage, and cardamom the best, although they can be a bit difficult to find. Parsley is a great revitalizer, with a lot of energy. The scent is unusual. Sage has a clearing effect that seems to be particularly effective when you are on a slide into despair, feeling overwhelmed and out of control. Cardamom is refreshing and particularly effective at clearing misery from your system, leaving you calm and relaxed.

Herbs can be your allies in helping fight stress, flushing toxins from the body, and combating adrenaline overload, all while supporting your physical health. Here are the five of the best herbs to reduce stress and the effects of stress:

- **Red Clover** (*Trifolium pratense*). My mother first introduced me to red clover as part of her "Cure What Ails Ya" tea when I was a teenager, and I make a batch of that tea every winter, both to gift and to drink. Red clover contains isoflavones, plant-based chemicals that produce estrogen-like effects in the body.[1] These isoflavones have been associated with an increase in HDL (aka "good") cholesterol in women. Women with a history of breast cancer may want to moderate their red clover intake.

- **Chamomile** (*Matricaria chamomilla*). Chamomile has antibacterial and sedative properties. The tea also increases glycine, an amino acid that relieves muscle spasms. Glycine also acts as a nerve relaxant, making the tea a mild sedative. One study found that chamomile may have modest benefits for some people with mild to moderate General Anxiety Disorder (GAD).[2] Some people may be allergic to chamomile, particularly if they are allergic to ragweed—test before ingesting.

- **Dill** (*Anethum graveolens*). Dill is one of the best herbs to use when experiencing stomach upset, a common side effect of stress. The seed smells good, prevents gas, produces urine, increases breast milk, increases alertness, and improves stomach functioning.[3] Add it to your food and enjoy its benefits.

- **Sage** (*Salvia officinalis*). Sage enhances memory and may be beneficial in treating patients with mild to moderate Alzheimer's disease.[4] It has also been shown to reduce cholesterol.[5] Finally, a cream containing sage (and rhubarb) extract was as effective as a prescription medicine in eliminating cold sores.[6]

- **St. John's Wort** (*Hypericum formosum*). St. John's wort is fairly well known for its ability to treat clinical depression (a common side effect of stress) in many cases.[7] Unfortunately, this herb has a lot of negative interactions with other herbs and medications, so be very careful when using this herb and absolutely involve your doctor in the process.

The best way to use these herbs is to cook with them or make teas. Herbal supplements are available, although they can be quite pricey.

Remedies for Emotional Excess

Stress and negative emotions are inextricably linked; stress often leads to anxiety, depression, and that insipid feeling of helplessness. Stress can make you feel like you are tightly wound and ready to snap if the pressure increases even a little bit. It may also cause a sense of paralysis or being fallow and unable to create. Research has consistently shown that stress, no matter how it manifests, causes specific physiological changes. In prehistoric times, these physical changes were essential for survival, and even now the stress response can be an asset for raising levels of performance during

critical events, such as a sports activity, an important meeting, or situations of actual danger or crisis.

When stress becomes persistent and low-level, however, it can do physical or psychological damage. Stress activates the adrenal glands, producing the hormone cortisol, which helps with the fight-or-flight response that is our reaction to stress. When we experience chronic stress, however, cortisol in the bloodstream leads to a variety of problems, including impaired cognitive performance, higher blood pressure, lowered immunity and inflammatory responses in the body, and increased abdominal fat.[8]

One of my favorite de-stressors is probably a real annoyance to my neighbors: loud music and dancing. I have a CD compilation I've created specifically to lift my mood and move my body. I turn the stereo up as loud as I can stand (my pets flee) and let the music wash through me and over me, moving my body as it desires. Relatedly, powerful drumming is an ancient technique for driving out demons and achieving a deep trance state. I can't help but think that those deep, pounding rhythms are perfect for driving out the demon of depression.

Meditation is another way to reduce stress, requiring only a bit of privacy, quiet, and time. Meditation, specifically the technique called "relaxation response," produces a state of deep relaxation in which our breathing, pulse rate, blood pressure, and metabolism are decreased. The technique consists of the silent repetition of a word, sound, or phrase while sitting quietly with eyes closed for 10 to 20 minutes and breathing through your nose in a free and natural way. You can choose any word or phrase you like. You can use a sound (such as "om"), a word (such as "one" or "peace"), or a word with special meaning to you. Intruding worries or thoughts should be ignored or dismissed to the best of your ability by focusing on the repetition. It's okay to open your eyes to look at a clock while you are practicing, but do not set an alarm.

When you have fin-ished, remain seated, first with your eyes closed and then with your eyes open, and gradually allow your thoughts to return to everyday reality. I have taught this technique to many people over the years, and every single one was able to do it. One mother of three small children used to retreat to the bathroom for her ten minutes, as it was a place guaranteed to provide privacy.

Self-grooming is a powerful natural stress-relief mechanism that can be profoundly soothing. Universally, grooming behavior is used by mammals to create intimacy, reinforce social networks, and release stress. Brushing or combing the hair significantly lowers stress, especially if it is done for a longer than normal period of time. (For those of us with short hair, stroking the scalp produces the same effect.) A variant is to sit down, hanging the head down while rubbing the pads of your fingers over the scalp in a slow, circular motion. Stroking your arms in slow, deliberate manner is also stress-reducing.

General Gimmicks for De-Stressing

There are a number of de-stressing techniques that are good for any kind of stress.

Deep breathing, the same in-through-the-nose and out-through-the-mouth technique often used to induce meditation, can work wonders and can be done anywhere. If you feel overwhelmed, close your eyes and spend several minutes focusing on nothing but your breathing. With each inhalation, imagine the air expanding your lungs and flowing into every part of your body. As you exhale, visualize any tension being released from you like poisonous gas.

Daydreaming is a wonderful way to change your stressful state. Begin with a few deep breaths, then start to fantasize about whatever will make you happiest in that moment. Be promoted to the job you covet, or take those extra bows on the stage at Carnegie Hall. Walk on a mountaintop, or fly through the clouds. Knowing you have this escape hatch to a better place open to you at any time can make even the most miserably stressful situation more bearable.

Grounding by collecting scattered energies and connecting to the comforting stability of Mother Earth can greatly reduce stress. Ideally you'll be able to actually touch the ground during exercise, but any place where you can stand still for a few minutes will do. Visualize all your stress collecting in the center of your body, and then push it out of you into Mother Earth.

Salt and water combined with intent make for a simple "wash" to pour over your feet and hands. This cleans the energy points found in the palms of the hands and the soles of the feet. If you are feeling particularly daunted, try swiping your saltwater hands across your brow—cleansing the third eye—or adding salt to your bath water and immersing yourself in it completely.

Take a bath. Once a week, add a handful of Epsom salt, 10 drops of essential oil (my recommendations were given earlier), and ½ cup baking soda to your hot bath. Stir deosil with intent to dissolve. Sit in the bath for at least 20 minutes, visualizing toxins leaving your body and feeling balance returning to your life.

Yoga is a wonderful way to reduce stress. Here are a few postures that anyone can do, almost anywhere:

- Lie on the floor, buttocks up against a wall, legs extended up the wall (you'll look like an "L"). Put your hands on your belly or rest them on the mat above your head. Close your eyes, relax your jaw, and drop your chin slightly. Breathe deeply and slowly in this position for 3 to 10 minutes.

- Lie on the floor, with knees bent a comfortable distance from your buttocks. Tilt your hips just slightly—it should feel relaxing—so that your back is mostly flat on the floor. Breathe deeply in this position for 10 to 20 minutes. (I combine this posture with meditation.)

A Spell Against Stress

Repeat calmly, letting it ease tension from your body and producing a deep sense of relaxation:

Storms within
Storms without
Storms above
Storms below
Calm in my center
There I will go
This is my will
And it is so.

. . . .

Stress can be overwhelming, but de-stressing doesn't have to be. I wish you a return to health and comfort!

NOTES

1. *University of Maryland Medical Center,* "Red Clover," http://www.umm.edu/altmed/articles/red-clover-000270.htm.

2. J. Amsterdam, L. Yimei, I. Soeller, et al., "A randomized, Double-Blind, Placebo-Controlled Trial of Oral *Matricaria recutita* (Chamomile) Extract Therapy for Generalized Anxiety Disorder," *Journal of Clinical Psychopharmacology* 29, no. 4 (August 2009):378–82.

3. L. Hornok, ed., *Cultivation and Processing of Medicinal Plants* (New York: John Wiley & Sons, 1992).

4. S. Akhondzadeh, et al., "*Salvia officinalis* Extract in the Treatment of Patients with Mild to Moderate Alzheimer's Disease," *Journal of Clinical Pharmaceutical Therapy* 28 (February 2003):53–59.

5. S. Kianbakht, et al., "Antihyperlipidemic Effects of *Salvia officinalis* L. Leaf Extract in Patients with Hyperlipidemia," *Phytotherapy Research* 25, no. 12 (December 2011): 1849–53.

6. R. Saller, et al., "Combined Herbal Preparation for Topical Treatment of *Herpes labialis," Forsch Komplementarmed Klass Naturheilkd* 8, no. 6 (December 2001):373–82.

7. Alan L. Miller, ND, "St. John's Wort (*Hypericum perforatum*): Clinical Effects on Depression and Other Conditions," *Alternative Medicine Review* 3, no. 1 (1998):18–26, http://www.thorne.com/altmedrev/.fulltext/3/1/18.pdf.

8. *University of Maryland Medical Center*, "Stress," http://www.umm.edu/patiented/articles/what_stress_000031_1.htm.

Lisa Mc Sherry *is a priestess and author living in the Pacific Northwest with her husband and three fur-children. She has a blog at www.cybercoven. org, leads JaguarMoon coven (www.jaguarmoon.com), and runs the review site Facing North (www.facingnorth.net).*

Illustrator: Rik Olson

Everybody's Working for the Weekend

Deborah Lipp

In the Pagan community, there is an ongoing dispute between those who choose to celebrate holidays on the "right" day and those who choose to celebrate holidays on the nearest convenient weekend. While tension exists, there isn't a whole lot of discussion as to theological, cultural, or ritual reasons; there's maybe some eye-rolling over differing opinions, but that's about it. What I'd like to do here is talk about some of these issues. In the course of this discussion, we'll be looking at what a Pagan might mean by doing something "the right way," and we'll also be exploring the notion of a Pagan work ethic.

When Pagans celebrate a "right" day that is *not* a weekend, they often need to take time off from work. Obviously, some people don't have jobs outside the home, and some people work on weekends, and so on, but most Americans work Monday through Friday with weekends off, and that's what we're going to assume for this article.

> ...there's an underlying tension between work and ritual; you sacrifice one for the other. Either you work when you "should" be doing ritual, or you do ritual when you should be working.

The point is, regardless of what your particular work schedule is, there's an underlying tension between work and ritual; you sacrifice one for the other. Either you work when you "should" be doing ritual, or you do ritual when you should be working. One or the other gets pushed off.

Cultural Background

In the West, we equate taking time off from work with religious observance. Christianity and Judaism both have a wide range of restrictions regarding labor on the Sabbath.

Many communities in the United States still have "blue laws"—laws designed for observing the Sabbath. As our society has become more pluralistic, these laws have mostly lifted, but they still exist in a patchwork of local ordinances, state liquor laws, and the like. Shopping, drinking, and various kinds of work are restricted on Sundays.

Christian observance of the Sabbath derives from the biblical description of the Sabbath as a day of rest, and the commandment to observe the Sabbath and keep it holy. It's rooted in Jewish law, which restricts a very wide range of activities on the Sabbath, even including, for the Orthodox, the use of electricity.

The upshot of all of this is that we tend to equate keeping a religious event holy with not working. Even if we are not Christians or Jews, and even if we weren't raised in religious families, we nonetheless absorb this as the norm from our culture, and it's reinforced every time we can't buy whisky or lumber on a Sunday. Sacred days, this tells us, are honored by refraining from doing what we do on ordinary days.

But is work something you do when you're not being religious? The cultural norm is, the religious day comes and therefore we stop work. But this is not necessarily the only way that work and ritual can be balanced. Perhaps it's not the *Pagan* way of doing things.

What Defines the "Right" Day?

There are a lot of ways to do ritual well. There are also quite a lot of ways to do it badly. Many of us come from backgrounds that teach us there is only one right way—to worship, to believe, to behave. Deviations are unacceptable or even damning. Many come to Paganism for the freedom first of all, but some confuse *many* right ways with the idea that all ways are equally right.

Look at it this way: You may have been taught that the only acceptable way to drink water is from an eight-ounce glass. You may find it freeing to discover that a four-ounce glass, or a teacup, or a mug, or a bottle, all work equally well. But that doesn't mean that pouring water into your cupped hands is as efficient (although it will work in a pinch), and it doesn't mean that pouring water onto your feet will work at all.

When talking about moons, the right day is easily defined. A full moon lasts for three days. All of the scientifically measurable effects of a full moon—from crime statistics to surgical outcomes to the mating habits of fish—occur from the day before full through the day after full. Since these are effects we experience, see with the naked eye, and process in our minds and bodies, it makes little sense to do a full moon rite outside of that three-day window. So, let's set aside moons and talk about holidays.

Pagan holidays are marked in a variety of ways, depending upon the specific branch of Paganism and the specific holiday, but they're going to fall into a few categories:

- An astronomical event (for example, a solstice or equinox)

- A seasonal event (for example, the beginning of winter or the longest day of the year)

- An agricultural or husbandry event (for example, first planting or first harvest)

- A commemorative event (for example, the feast day of a deity or the anniversary of something)

I'm going to set aside commemorative events as out of the scope of this article, because the other three are pretty obviously interrelated, and because the variety of commemorative celebrations is so huge that there are probably as many exceptions as rules.

The other three may not seem all that different, at first. Isn't the vernal equinox an astronomical event and also the beginning of spring (a seasonal event) and also the beginning of spring planting (agricultural)? While these are related, they are not identical, and what makes the day the "right" day is different in each case.

Why Is That Day Right?

ASTRONOMICAL

In some cases, the astronomical event is precisely what is being marked, and in this case, there is no room for variance. The ray of light that penetrates the secret chamber at the moment of sunrise on the summer solstice can be observed only at that moment and no other. There are certainly Pagan traditions where those exact events are the defining feature of a holiday ritual, but I'd argue that in many cases, the astronomical event simply *coincides* with a seasonal or agricultural occurrence.

The thing is, a lot of solar and planetary astronomy isn't felt in our day-to-day lives with the immediacy or intensity of lunar changes. I'm not arguing that they don't affect us—they absolutely do!—but the impact, compared to a full or new moon, is more like a light sprinkle than a downpour.

What is the lore associated with your tradition's ritual for an event? It is often disconnected from the sun and stars, and instead is concerned with the experience of seasons, of weather, of crops, and of the flow of life. I'd argue that if you're talking about, and celebrating, the flow of life, then acknowledging work schedules is part of that flow.

SEASONAL

There's a kind of seasonality that we feel as part of ordinary, day-to-day life. I used to live in a town that didn't allow overnight on-street parking during the part of the year when snow removal might be necessary. The signs around town said, "No Overnight Parking, November through April." In other words, Samhain to Beltane. There are innumerable such small examples—from school schedules to street fairs, from insect invasions to cleaning the chimney—of ways that changes in the seasons touch our mundane lives. Indeed, one of the purposes of most seasonal Pagan holidays is to attune ourselves more closely with these changes, and as we become more attuned, we become more aware of the way the seasons already affect us.

One thing these examples demonstrate is that seasonal changes are both natural and social. We know that summer officially starts at the summer solstice around June 21 and ends on the fall equinox around September 21, but most Americans think of summer as running from Memorial Day (end of May) to Labor Day (beginning of September). If summer is the "let's go to the beach" season, then the social dates make a lot of sense.

A season might also, of course, begin with a natural sign—like the blooming of the crocuses or the first sighting of a robin indicating the onset of spring.

Ritual celebrations that commemorate seasons can resonate more deeply by pulling in information from the local culture. For instance, at my Yule rites, I like to make mention of the holiday lights hanging everywhere, and incorporate them into the seasonal motif of the returning light and striking a light against the darkness.

What's the right day for a seasonal celebration? On those occasions where it coincides with a secular or community celebration, it might make sense to do it then. Lining up your Yule celebration with Christmas Eve means there is no work conflict (although there is often family conflict). Notice that this requires celebrating the season and not the astronomy.

Most seasonal events take place in a date range, but some are more anchored to a specific day. If you are marking Yule as the longest night of the year, there is only one night that fits the bill. As with an astronomically based rite, you need to celebrate *that* day. However, there's no reason you can't mark, for example, "the season of darkness, when nights are longest."

Seasons, as we've seen, are connected to both nature and society. In society, people work, and work is valued. Seasons create a kind of breathing room, where we work and rest, work and rest, in an inhale-exhale pattern. I've already described summer in terms of vacation time. Since we mark time by the activities in our lives, it makes sense that our ritual occasions coincide with those ebbs and flows and cycles.

AGRICULTURAL AND HUSBANDRY

By far, the most common associations of Pagan holidays, especially Wiccan ones, fall into this category. Oimelc (February 2), we are told, is when sheep begin to lactate. There are planting festivals, harvest festivals, corn festivals, and wheat festivals. A wealth of spiritual metaphor is found in rising and falling, feasting and renewing, becoming fertile and falling fallow.

Why are agricultural cycles so important? In part, it's because they dominate life. You can't schedule a harvest; when the plants are ripe, you bring them in or risk losing them entirely. In this way, agriculture schedules you, not the other way around. In part, it's because these cycles are rooted in the land on which you live. They are natural, immediate, palpable, and easy to uncover, even if you live in the city or the suburbs. Also, they really are the root of life. We all have to eat; it's as simple as that. Nature expresses herself most ferociously and most generously in her growth and dearth, rain and drought, abundance and paucity. There's no question that even the most urban of Pagans can, and usually do, deepen their connection to life by paying attention to plant and animal cycles.

Now, here's the thing about agricultural festivals: They occur because work is finished. They occur when they have to. The crop is ready to be brought in, so you, and perhaps your entire community, work your tail(s) off bringing the crop in. Then you have a feast. You have a feast partially because there are piles and piles of food around—food you just harvested. That food has to be prepared— canned, jarred, pickled, dried, or whatever—so some portion of it is simply cooked and served, and it's time to eat like royalty. Feast!

At the opposite end of the spectrum is planting. You get those seeds planted as soon as you can. You don't wait for a convenient time. As soon as the ground is ready, in they go, because time is food. When the planting is done, you're exhausted and you rest. Time for a day off!

Both planting and harvesting can be surrounded by ritual activity, and have been since the dawn of civilization. Seeds must be blessed and their growth must be encouraged. Fields emptied of the harvest must be made ready for next year's crop, the Gods should be thanked for the harvest, and the harvest must be blessed with the ability to sustain the community. Here we see how a holiday celebration naturally flows out of work: Work ends, and ritual and feasting begin.

If your work is in an office or at a factory, it's still work, and it's still true that its natural cessation—a cessation demanded by the work and not, or not often, by you—is when it's time to celebrate and to ritually mark that celebration.

A Pagan Work Ethic

To me, a truly Pagan life flow is found in the agricultural and animal husbandry style of celebration: When work is done, feasts begin, and when feasting (and recovery) ends, it's time for work again. Work pulls us in, demands of us, and then releases us.

Judaism and Christianity teach us to impose an order from above, to force a separation of work and ritual. That idea permeates Western culture, and perhaps it infects our ritual life needlessly. There are certainly times when nature demands we stop what we're doing and pay attention to ritual, but there are also times when she requires that we stop what we're doing and pay attention to work.

A Pagan work ethic, it seems to me, arises from the idea that we do what is needed when it is needed. It arises, most importantly, from the notion of a balanced life in which artificial and external separations have no place. Many of us, when we first became Pagan, were blown away by the integration of pleasure and sacredness. Our culture separates these things with a firm wall: Hedonism is the opposite of piety. Sex, imbibing, and even eating are all sinful to a greater or lesser extent (every pleasure seems to have a "deadly sin" associated with it: Gluttony, Lust, Sloth…). Some religions restrict pleasure so profoundly that even singing or bright colors are avoided.

> **A Pagan work ethic, it seems to me, arises from the idea that we do what is needed when it is needed. It arises, most importantly, from the notion of a balanced life in which artificial and external separations have no place.**

As Pagans, we learn that nature is good, our bodies are good, and pleasure is good. In Wicca, the Goddess tells us: "All acts of love and pleasure are My rituals." Once we start thinking of a Pagan life as one in which the walls of division between "religion" and "life" are broken down, we begin to see that the same principle can be applied to work. Just as a harvest is sacred, so is putting food on the table through other means. When work ceases, it's time to play, and have a holiday.

It's for these reasons that I'm comfortable, theologically, with holding a sabbat on the nearest available Saturday.

Ritual Structure

I'm comfortable with that theologically, but what about ritually? There are serious ritual considerations once you choose to shift a date from the traditional one.

Too many times I've stood in a circle on the Saturday three days before the summer solstice and heard the Priestess intone, "Today is the longest day of the year." Um, no. It is the season of long days, and you can say that. Or you can say that you're commemorating the longest day, which is about to occur. Or you can talk about summer and long days in more general terms.

Here's a fundamental ritual principle: Refrain from lying to your psyche if you want your psyche to be cooperative. When your mind hears something it knows to be false, you are thrown out of the mental state most conducive to ritual. You cease to suspend disbelief. Your energy is compromised.

Another thing to keep in mind is the way in which energy cycles. Peaks are approached with slow, mounting energy, which we might call induction, or anticipation, or buildup, or foreplay. When those peaks are achieved, drop-off tends to be rapid.

Suppose, for example, you are doing sex magic. The moment of orgasm is the perfect moment to send your energy into your spell, but that's a hard moment to capture exactly. Right *before* orgasm, you're full of that nearly-there fever of excitement. Right *after* orgasm, you're done, spent, nodding off, or catching a smoke. Once a magical moment—whatever that moment happens to be—is reached, the buildup of energy dissipates quickly.

For this reason, you can best take advantage of the astronomical and seasonal powers of a sabbat on the convenient weekend before rather than after it occurs. After the summer solstice, the solstice energy will be crumbling, and the season leading into Lammas has begun.

· · · · · · · · · · · · ·

I can summarize my thoughts, then, as follows:

- Determine why you're celebrating: Is it astronomy, the season, or agriculture that informs your rite?

- Consider a truly Pagan work ethic that incorporates a work/life balance and recognizes the sacredness of putting food on the table.

- Construct rituals consistent with the actual date on which the celebration occurs.

- If you are not celebrating on a significant day, before is better than after.

Blessed be.

Deborah Lipp *is the author of six books, including* Merry Meet Again: Lessons, Life & Love on the Path of a Wiccan High Priestess *and* The Elements of Ritual: Air, Fire, Water and Earth in the Wiccan Circle. *Deborah has been Wiccan for over 30 years, and a High Priestess of the Gardnerian tradition since 1986. She's been published in* newWitch, Llewellyn's Magical Almanac, Pangaia, Green Egg, *and* The Druid's Progress. *Deborah is also an avid media writer and blogger, and is co-owner of* Basket of Kisses: Smart Discussion About Smart Television (*www.lippsisters.com*). *She lives in Rockland County, New York.*

Illustrator: Jennifer Hewitson

Drawing Out Magic

Lexa Olick

No one has ever underestimated the power of hands. They are truly amazing instruments. Not only are they physical tools, but they are emotional tools as well. When we see a clenched fist, we instantly identify it with anger. An outstretched palm is usually associated with begging, and we always shake hands as an immediate gesture of friendship. While we sometimes try to conceal our emotions by hiding our eyes or watching our posture, there's too much energy and emotion flowing through our hands to ever fully be concealed.

Pressure, curves, and the complexity of drawings or words can reveal images in our mind that are not easy to express vocally. The energy behind these nonverbal representations can be harnessed for magical use.

Hands have a nonverbal language of their own that is seen not only by our actions, but also by the way we write lines on a page. Pressure, curves, and the complexity of drawings or words can reveal images in our mind that are not easy to express vocally. The energy behind these nonverbal representations can be harnessed for magical use.

For centuries, art has been linked to magic. It is especially linked to sympathetic magic, which can be seen in North American rock art. Shamans would carve images into stone tablets to cause droughts for their enemies. The only way to put an end to the droughts was to discover the tablets and throw them into water. The droughts were then instantly replaced with rainstorms.

Even though it's called rock art, it was not always found on rocks or cave walls. Sometimes a need for magic or illustration was more spontaneous. A shaman either did not have the time to find a better location or was instantly compelled to draw an image at that specific moment. Many times, an image was drawn in dirt. The shaman would pick up a nearby stick and suddenly drop to his knees to carve an idea into the ground.

Even nonrepresentational motifs were created for purposes of sympathetic magic. It was the energy and thought behind the designs that fueled their goals. Today, one of the most common free-form methods of expression is doodling. Since the hands attract and direct magic, every squiggle has a purpose. These drawings, no matter how rushed, have unique and personal meanings as well as magical origins. Doodles may seem like inexplicable marks, but with closer inspection, we see that these random drawings are full of honesty. We are not concerned about hiding our emotions or

thoughts when we are just drawing to pass the time. Since they are produced while the focus of our attention is elsewhere, the images created are those buried within our subconscious. It's very similar to visions in a dream, and just like dreams, we must first interpret those drawings before we put them to magical use.

Doodling is a playful and creative activity. There's no pressure when it comes to scribbling, so doodles create a safe environment for us to visually explore our thoughts. It creates a visual solution similar to a math equation. In fact, math plays a significant role in doodling. Geometric shapes are usually the basis of both simple and elaborate drawings. Many people begin by drawing a single pyramid. Once that simple shape is formed, it's easy to get lost in how many triangles you can fit inside that first pyramid.

The ancient Egyptians believed that the earth was created from a great mound, which they represented with a pyramid shape. With a history like that, it's no wonder triangles are a symbol for aspiration. They also represent ambition. The cone is similar in shape to a triangle, and the dunce cap was originally thought to stimulate the brain. Triangles show a desire to advance in life. If you include triangles in your doodles, it means that you are dedicated to your goals and look forward to what is to come. A triangle that points upward looks similar to the blade of an athame. Since its highest point is directed upward, it symbolizes the determination to achieve goals.

Triangles are used to form talismans such as hexagrams, pentacles, or triquetras. They also represent each of the four elements. An upward-pointing triangle symbolizes fire. If it has a horizontal line, then it represents air. A downward-pointing triangle symbolizes water. If that has a horizontal line, then it represents earth. All these triangles combined make up the points of a hexagram.

While the ancient Egyptians thought the earth was formed from a giant mound, they also believed the triangular shape represented the sun's rays. Another shape commonly associated with the sun or earth is the circle. Circles have no beginning or end. They are limitless and symbols of completeness and eternity. It's hard to draw a perfect circle. In fact, it's downright frustrating, if that is your goal. However, when circles are drawn idly on a whim, it usually indicates a moment of contentment. Using circles for talismans is a good idea because they're filled with positive energy.

Triangles and circles are simple shapes that branch out and become more detailed drawings. The same is true for rectangles and squares. Geometric shapes represent the logical mind. They reveal the ability to think, assess, and plan ahead. Hex signs, which have been used for centuries as talismans, are created from geometric shapes. As a whole, they are circular, but their inner design takes all shapes. It wouldn't be difficult to borrow a doodle and transform it into a unique hex sign. Large drawings can be cut away from the page and découpaged onto wooden plaques for wall hangings. Since they're flat, the plaques can also slide underneath mattresses for prophetic dreams. Small drawings can similarly be découpaged onto one-inch wooden circles to create coins to carry around in purses or pockets.

Probably the most recognizable geometric figure in Paganism is the pentacle. It's evenly balanced and perfectly designed. Heinrich

Agrippa's pentagram illustrates the harmony in the universe and the human body. It's a great example of the logical mind at work. The balance seen in a pentacle or pentagram is also seen in our random scribbling. Doodles can extend throughout a page or hide tightly in a corner. Large markings dominate a page the same way a person takes charge of a room. Large doodles that extend throughout a sheet of paper suggest that the person is outgoing and confident. Such people are as lively in life as they are in their scribbling. The smaller drawings that huddle close together in the corner of a page suggest that the person likes to keep a low profile and revel in some quiet time. These people are just as contained as their drawings. They tuck themselves away in a corner and out of sight.

Straight lines can also hide themselves. If doodling on lined paper, it's common to trace the lines that are already established before branching out into full-blown drawing. Straight lines express a need to be in control. If you find yourself drawing straight lines, it means you have a sense of order that cannot be deviated from. You're not interested in exploration or experimentation. You would rather plan ahead and stay organized.

Horizontal lines represent a path. They are symbolic of the dual nature of humanity, such as good and evil, beginning to end, and male and female. Vertical lines represent the body and are suggestive of trees. The tree of life shows the connection of all creation. While there's no specific order to the tree of life, it shows that everything has its place in the world and everything is connected.

Curvy lines follow no plan. People who are spontaneous or imaginative enjoy the free-flowing movement of wavy lines. They accept things as they come and continue to draw freely.

How lines are drawn is also important. Some are rushed, while others are deliberate. The pressure of the pencil on the paper is revealing as well. A pencil dug into the page or harsh, repetitive shading shows frustration or worry. If keeping drawings for magical works, it's best to choose ones created with positive energy. Light shading and graceful lines are positive responses to feeling relaxed, and show that you are kind and sensitive. Those are emotions that you hopefully want to keep for magic work.

When it comes to spellwork, having the right mindset is important. Therefore, it is wise to save drawings that encourage the right attitude. While performing spells, you should be filled with confidence. Keep the drawings that were created while feeling relaxed, safe, and comfortable.

Lexa Olick *is the author of* Witchy Crafts: 60 Enchanted Projects for the Creative Witch, *published by Llewellyn. When she is not writing, painting, or teaching, she enjoys quiet evenings at home in her tiny house with an even tinier dog.*

Illustrator: Tim Foley

Expanding Your Circle: Thoughts on Finding Community

Blake Octavian Blair

The desire to find community is a natural instinct. We all want to have the support, fellowship, assistance, and nurturing that a group of like-minded individuals can provide. For many Pagans, however, this presents a bit of a challenge. Those lucky enough to live in large urban centers are likely to be blessed with public Pagan groups and shops, making it easy to locate your fellow magickal folk. Furthermore, the larger public Pagan presence can make for a more welcoming climate in which to be out of the broom closet.

However, for many Pagans, knowing where to start to locate and get involved in the community can be overwhelming. Practitioners living in more rural or religiously conservative areas, such as the southern United States and/or the Bible Belt, may have a bit more challenging experience when trying to find a sense of community in which they feel they genuinely fit. This task can potentially feel very daunting and be severely dampening to one's spirit. This can prove to be true not only if you have always lived in such an area but alternatively if you have had to relocate to such an area. This scenario can be particularly frustrating if the area you left behind had a thriving and open community. But have no fear: there are several ways you can expand your circle and broaden your search. You may find a community of like-minded individuals happily waiting to be discovered in an area you never thought to look. You may even grow and expand your knowledge in the process—always a welcome side effect!

If for whatever reason you need to stay low-key or in the broom closet, you still need not go without like-minded community. To some degree you can have your cakes and ale and eat them too. In fact, the places to look for like-minded folks are essentially the same as those for out-of-the-closet Pagans. Pagans are known for being resourceful people!

Reiki and energy healing groups and exchanges are an often overlooked and unexpected place to find magickally minded folk. And upon second thought, one realizes that this is in fact a perfectly logical place to find metaphysically minded people. I myself am a Reiki Master/Teacher and even in the South, I have been able to find Pagan, Pagan-friendly, and shamanically minded folks at Reiki shares. There is a large overlap among these communities, and you will meet many people who practice Witchcraft and magick there who may not in turn attend a public gathering openly designated to be for Witches and Pagans. You may attend an energy healing exchange and wonder how you didn't find these kindred sooner, seemingly hiding in plain sight!

Additionally, many areas that seem devoid of Pagan activity have thriving shamanic communities. I've participated in rituals held in fairly public spaces and performed in various styles, including Native (North) American, Peruvian Shamanic, and modern Neopagan style, and oddly, I heard little outside inquiry beyond, "What are you burning?" The curious bystander was satisfied with the answer, "White sage, for energetic purification and cleansing. It is a common practice among Native American cultures."

Interestingly, it does seem that in more religiously conservative areas, practices that pay homage to Native American traditions are accepted without question despite the fact that many Native traditions clearly have shared ritual and theological elements with Paganism and Witchcraft. However, if drawing upon such traditions, it is important to do so with proper research and giving due respect to those cultures.

Shamanic practitioners come from almost every faith and culture from around the globe. You will find Christians, Buddhists, Pagans, and those practicing various indigenous paths all gathered together at many community shamanic ceremonies for a common goal. Almost always, the people that gather at this type of environment, if not Pagan, will be extremely Pagan-friendly, with many beliefs in common. I met a good friend of mine at a Reiki share at my Reiki instructor's home. He identifies himself as a "Shamanic Buddhist Quaker." As diverse as that title is, and as different as it is from the title that I identify with, we have a great deal in common and have done many a ceremony and ritual working with each other and have a number of incredibly similar beliefs.

Finding a metaphysical-related book club is another good bet. Pagans have a long-standing reputation as bibliophiles, and many

proudly self-proclaim the title. Book clubs with such a focus may not appear easy to find. However, try doing some Internet research, checking bookstore bulletin boards, and visiting your local metaphysical or New Age shop if you are lucky enough to have one.

Unitarian Universalist (UU) churches often have a diverse plethora of groups, activities, and book clubs because their congregations are often made up of members from many different backgrounds and traditions. Pay a visit to your local UU chuch and inquire if they have a healing, metaphysical, or New Age group. You may get lucky and find they have a local chapter of the Covenant of Unitarian Universalist Pagans (CUUPS). One of the perks of this situation is that the group is provided with a relatively safe environment to hold its gatherings in.

If you strike out in trying to locate any of the types of groups I've talked about so far, there is always the option of starting your own.

If you plan on organizing [your own] group, it may be wise to hold your first few meetings in a public setting until you are comfortable enough inviting people into your home. Parks, coffee shops, bookstores, and diners are all potential options.

There are many websites, including The Witches' Voice (witchvox.com) and Meetup (meetup.com), that will allow you either for free or for a small fee to post a listing to help organize such a group. Many of these groups meet at members' homes. If you plan on organizing such a group, it may be wise to hold your first few meetings in a public setting until you are comfortable enough inviting people into your home. Parks, coffee shops, bookstores, and diners are all potential options. This can be especially important if you are unsure how they may react to the three-foot-tall Bast statue on your fireplace mantle! Remember, not everybody interested in these topics comes from a background that held Witchcraft and Paganism in an affirming light. They may not be close-minded; however, a more subtle first encounter isn't necessarily a bad precaution in conservative cultural climates.

There is always the possibility of meeting a like-minded soul on an individual basis seemingly through serendipity and happenstance. You may be checking out at the local grocery store and do a double take, noticing that the cashier has a pentacle pendant on their necklace. This very thing actually occurred to me shortly after moving to my current location while shopping at our local co-op. Coffee shops that attract an alternative customer base are also places you may fare well for such a happenstance discovery. You may notice that the patron a few tables over or across the shop has a stylish triple-goddess sticker on her laptop. Remember, just because a person openly displays a Pagan-related symbol doesn't always mean they are thoroughly public with their beliefs. People often don't notice what isn't pointed out to them, and many Pagan symbols can go unnoticed to an untrained eye. Pagans in less tolerant areas often use this fact to great advantage. On the other hand, such environments are often about social interaction, so perhaps you might start some casual con-

versation before broaching the topic in hopes of making a new friend.

Some of us are very open about our Pagan beliefs and are far out of the broom closet and in the public eye as teachers, healers, tarot readers, and authors. However, it is understandable that not all Pagan folk are in a position to be so open about their beliefs. It is also important to remember that not every person with an interest in metaphysics, nature, or alternative spirituality is open to Pagan-related paths. In fact, you may well encounter people who are less than approving or a bit skeptical of your path. If you are in a group or public setting and you are out of the broom closet, this is usually of little immediate hostile consequence. Most people are willing to overlook differences of opinion. However, if you are in the broom closet, you may want to be careful what you reveal about your personal practices and beliefs and stick to the common territory of the group's topic until you feel out the group's climate, become more comfortable, or make personal friends with individuals you come to know well enough that you feel relaxed in revealing more. It would not be advisable to walk in and proclaim, "I'm a Witch! Who else here practices Witchcraft? Esbat party, anyone?" Half the populace of a small town may know who the new neighborhood Witch is by the following sunrise. In many areas that can unfortunately result in negative consequences which can vary from minimal to severe and from social to physical.

If you are in a position at this time where you feel you cannot be out of the broom closet on any level for whatever reason, be it work-related, cultural climate, or personal comfort, you can still seek community online. While this does not have all the benefits that in-person community contact provides, it is considerably better than being totally alone. In recent years, with the upsurge of social networking sites, we have seen the creation of sites like Pagan Space (www.paganspace.net), which is essentially the Pagan answer to sites like Facebook or MySpace (which both have huge Pagan populations of their own). While with an online community you may not be able to hold a Pagan movie night or full moon ritual at a group member's home, there are a few advantages. You can still have community moral support, share healing requests, spell tips, and ritual ideas, and even coordinate synchronized spell-working with other members. You can choose to what degree you want to be out of the broom closet and, if needed, you can maintain your anonymity through the use of an online screen name. If down the road things should change to where you are comfortable or in a position to meet others in person, most sites provide geographical information about their members, so you can network with those in your area.

It you are in the broom closet, it is important to identify your reasons why. I do not advocate that anyone live their life in fear. Perhaps you live in an extremely unaccepting area and you fear retaliation in the form of bullying, vandalism, being professionally ostracized, or worse. Keeping your witchiness low-key may be an intelligent choice in these situations and save you a considerable amount of worry.

However, if you choose to be out of the broom closet and open with your beliefs, and you've deemed the risk of doing so to be manageable, this is also a choice not to live in fear of what others think about you. As I mentioned earlier, the consequences of being public with your Paganism can be quite varied. What I do encourage anyone to do, no matter their broom closet status, is to live genuinely. Be yourself. There are ways to be discreet about your beliefs while not necessarily hiding or compromising them. It is important to remember that, on one hand, people's opinions of you are just that—their opinions. Take that for what it is worth. Depending on the situation, others' opinions may or may not have any bearing on you. If you feel your safety or security will be affected or threatened on any level, that is when to be cautious. Either choice—in or out of the broom closet—is valid and appropriate and must be arrived at on an individual basis. Just be genuine to yourself in how you live your life.

In addition to taking an active role in seeking out venues and opportunities to find community through gatherings and events, in person and online, you can also use your magickal skills to boost your community manifesting efforts. Try making a vision board, which is a collage made either by gluing images and words that represent and resonate with your goals, aspirations, and desires to a piece of

cardboard or posterboard, or by pinning them to a corkboard. The advantage of the corkboard method is that you can add, remove, take away, and rearrange elements. Essentially, the ritual act of its creation, and the completed board's vibration within your space, tell the universe what you want. Like attracts like.

Do you want a group to hold ritual with? Find an image of people holding circle. Do you want to meet others with an interest in Egyptian-slanted Paganism? Include a picture of Isis or a scarab. Witches into arts and crafts? Perhaps a picture of knitting needles and yarn. Friends interested in kitchen and garden witchery? Maybe a picture of someone tending an herb garden. If you yearn for the type of friends you can share anything with, you could print out and put the words "Sisterhood & Brotherhood" on the board. You get the idea.

Hang the vision board in a place in your home where you'd like to entertain company or have a gathering, such as a family room or in view of your kitchen table. (Guests seem to naturally gravitate to the kitchen table as a gathering spot. It has a magickal pull all its own!) Adjust the board's contents as necessary as your search unfolds and your results manifest.

In the modern age of the Craft, no matter what your situation or location, you need not be without community unless you so choose. Whether in person or online, it is my hope that, regardless of your location and situation, you can find a nurturing and supportive community in which you are comfortable participating and feel a sense of belonging.

Blake Octavian Blair (*Carrboro, NC*) *is an Eclectic Pagan Witch, ordained minister, psychic, tarot reader, freelance writer, Usui Reiki Master-Teacher, musical artist, and a devotee of Lord Ganesha. He holds a degree in English and Religion from the University of Florida. In his spare time he enjoys beading jewelry and knitting, and is an avid reader. Blake lives in the Piedmont region of North Carolina with his beloved husband, an aquarium full of fish, and an indoor jungle of houseplants. Visit him on the Web at www.blakeoctavianblair.com or write him at blake@blakeoctavianblair.com.*

Illustrator: Bri Hermanson

Cybermagic: Ancient Traditions in a Modern World

Jymi x/ø (Reverend Variable)

There is a growing contingent of magical folk who are bringing the old ways to a new frontier. We're finding new ways to apply age-old ideas, and as we take our first steps into a new realm, we are finding that our familiar gods and goddesses have been there waiting for us the whole time.

I have never felt such a deep connection with the universe as I do in my office late at night, sailing across the vast digital expanses of the Internet. Libraries, museums, galleries, and music halls are mine with just a few clicks. I can have a face-to-face conversation with a friend who lives thousands of miles away, or shop for magical wares from a craftsman in another state. Sometimes I gaze inward and use my computer to bring forth worlds of my own, shaping and guiding them as they take form on the screen before me.

The computer is our gateway to a whole new dimension.

Cyberspace

Cyberspace, cybermagic, techno-wizards—what exactly are we talking about?

Like the center of a charged circle, cyberspace is a dimension—a separate reality—made of energy and thought, generated by the minds and spirits of the people who work with it and within it. It is a state of being in which we agree that certain ideas and ways of experiencing things are real and valid, even if we can't actually touch them in the physical world (or "meatspace," as the cyber-slang goes). And like a circle, it can be generated by many people or just one. The participants may be working together via an Internet forum with thousands of members, or perhaps there's just one person fully engaged in an onscreen activity. If you've used a computer at all, even to play a little game of Solitaire, you've been in cyberspace.

Your Plastic Familiar

Many people don't think of a computer as having a "brain" or a "soul." While the machine may not be sentient in the same way that we humans are, there is a coherent, continuous awareness: it remembers things, seeks input, solves problems, and creates new internal connections from its experiences. Some would argue that the computer is only following its program, but if you want to get technical, human behavior can also be shown to be merely the result of a series of complicated programs. Does it matter? Spirit takes many forms. Why not welcome this little electronic creature as a magical ally? Give it a name. Say "hello" to it when you turn it on, and "thank you" when you turn it off. Learn about its abilities, needs, and preferences. Take responsibility for its health. You wouldn't let strangers threaten your animals or children, so don't leave your computer vulnerable to viruses and hackers. Things happen, but it's really not hard to prevent most of these mishaps.

Spirit takes many forms. Why not welcome this little electronic creature as a magical ally? Give it a name. Say "hello" to it when you turn it on, and "thank you" when you turn it off.

Once nice thing about a computer familiar is that when its shell becomes too old or infirm to carry on, its essence can be transferred to a new one. My own familiar, TORGO, is currently on his eighth incarnation. (We have both gained a lot of new power over the years!) He has a special "dedication" file that I wrote for him, and every time I upgrade or add a new machine to our network, the file goes in, alerting the "essence" of the computer—the energy that is my friend TORGO—that he has a new home. This isn't a complicated computer program. It's just a text file that I store in the system folder. If you can type and save a written page, you can do this, too!

Your computer system contains the essence of your entire digital history. It contains all the energy you've projected into your computers over the years. This isn't limited to one machine, either. Your familiar dwells within the files and processes of all the computers with which you become entangled, especially if they can share files. This entity lives in your desktop, your laptop, your smartphone, and maybe even your work computer.

Magical Correspondences for the Technomage

The world has changed a lot in just a few decades, let alone centuries. But look deeper, and you'll find that the same patterns keep repeating. There are plenty of old ideas embedded in the new technology.

These correspondences are entirely scalable: they can apply to one computer, a local network, or the entire Internet—and your relationship to these entities.

ELEMENTS

Earth: Earth is represented by the actual physical components of the computer.

Fire: Fire is the raw power of change—it gets things done. Fire corresponds to the electricity that lights up the system and makes it go.

Air: The logical, mental element refines the raw power and brings order to the energy flow. Air is represented by the mathematics and the codes that run the system and the software.

Water: Water is usually associated with emotions. If computers have emotional quality, we have yet to learn how to relate to them (other than our own emotional response when the computer does something unexpected). However, water is also associated with deep activity: dreams, the subconscious, and other activity going on beneath the surface. There are thousands of subprocesses going on within the system during any session. You'll never know about most of these, but their effects are essential to your work.

The water element also refers to a "flowing" quality. Water will take the path of least resistance, seek its own level, and carry along anything immersed within it. The watery nature of electronics shows in the way the force (fire) moves through the circuits, bringing impulses and info-laden bits and bytes along with it.

Spirit: As you enter information into your computer, your input is translated into something it can understand. When it responds, the machine code it generates is translated into something that you can understand. These connections depend on all of the other four elements working together, forming a bond between the human and the machine. When you venture into the Internet, you're in a world created by human minds and computers working together. Can you feel the "spirit" of the 'net as you explore the electronic pathways?

TOOLS

Many electronic devices correspond to basic magical tools, too.

Wand—Mouse: As you move your mouse with your hand, your cursor changes position on the screen, ready to direct your will.

Athame/Sword—Buttons: Once the energy is raised, we use the athame and the sword to issue commands and make changes. When you click on something, you are making choices and implementing your will. (When you start working with invocations in cyberspace, wave your "wand" to direct attention; but I don't recommend clicking on an entity on your screen unless invited. That's rude!)

Pentacle (the physical tool)—Mousepad: The mousepad is one of the main places where your body/mind interfaces with the computer's body/mind. Enhance its protective/grounding energies by choosing (or creating) a special design.

Chalice/Cauldron—Screen/Windows: The screen and the windows (that is, the boxes where you interact with your files, not the "Windows" operating system itself) are the sacred spaces in which you mix your materials, pour your energy, and watch your work come together.

Cords—Cords: Cybermages certainly have enough of these. More on electronic cord magic later.

Altar Cloth: Your desktop wallpaper is the first thing you see when you turn on the computer, and (usually) the last thing you see when you turn it off. Use a personal magical image for your desktop wallpaper: a photo of your physical altar, a sacred space that you've actually visited, or perhaps a painting you've made of a magical place you've seen in your dreams or visualizations. The point is to make a personal connection. There are a lot of "magic"-themed images available on the Internet, but using any of those is like throwing some mass-produced poster up in your most sacred chamber. Make this your own.

Book of Shadows: You're probably already using the computer to type a few notes, and maybe you even keep a digital journal by now. With a little extra effort, you can build an entire cross-referenced library of images, notes, indexes, lists—make your magical library and journals work together! (Look into HTML code or database programs like MS Access.) Magic is about making connections. Databases can be as simple or as complex as you're ready to make them, and they're invaluable for stepping back, looking at the big picture, and seeing connections where you may never have noticed them before.

Your Magical Parlor: When you're ready to take the next step, you can build your own digital "altar room." This can take many forms: websites can live on or off the Internet. You could show it off or require a password. There are a number of different options for creating your site: you might install a content management system like Word Press or Drupal, or, if you're so inclined, code it yourself. Create a Facebook page for your magical persona, or, if you're really eager to walk around in cyberspace, join a 3-D site like Second Life and start building! It doesn't have to be perfect or a marvel of technology. It just has to be yours, with your own touch.

- When performing spellwork with your computer, personalize your display to match your intent. Create a special "altar cloth" graphic design to use as your desktop wallpaper during the ritual, and if your operating system allows further customization, adjust your interface to a color scheme that corresponds to your magic.

- Use the computer to provide light, an animated magical graphic, or audio. If you like background music for your work, try your hand at creating an actual soundtrack, complete with bells, chanting, a guided meditation track, and any number of other components you can think of to include.

- Cybermagic is well suited for cord magic, as long as you apply a little common sense. Don't wear a cord that's plugged in if there's any chance that you or your equipment could come to harm. Obviously, the water element does not belong anywhere near live cords. With that in mind, though, how about some spells knotted into your main power outlet or co-axial cable?

- Have you ever tried divination by links? Think of a question, then start clicking random links. Don't think about it too much—just click from page to page. See where you end up.

The Cyber Coven

Web-savvy readers are probably familiar with many popular websites devoted to magic and magical practices. There's no shortage of magical material on the 'net, but you don't have to stop at just reading about it. If you enjoy working with a group, the computer can provide access to a vast magical community. (Jenett Silver provides excellent information

about connecting online in her article "Magic in the Net," in *Llewellyn's 2011 Witches' Companion*.)

Join a few of the forums, introduce yourself to the members, and soon you'll find that you're making friends from all over the world. If you and your friends want to try working a little magic together, there are plenty of ways to gather in cyberspace without traveling a single block in the physical world.

There are many video chat programs you could use. If your computer can't handle the graphics, simply make an agreement that you'll all meet on the astral plane at a certain time. (I was once a member of a group who practiced collaborative dreamwork. We had never met on the physical plane, but knew each other well in the astral. We used Internet forums to make plans and compare notes.)

. . . .

Our computers can be powerful magical partners and friends. We have a lot to learn from each other, and a lot that we can accomplish if we work together. Let's connect, and build a new world.

Reverend Jymi "Variable" x/ø *is good with shapes, words, sounds, light, shadows, numbers, and ideas. Her family consists of one excellent husband, a fine yellow snake, several computers, two sarcastic automobiles, the houseplants that she keeps finding by the dumpster whenever someone moves out of her apartment complex, and any spiders who happen to wander into the house. Her influences include Frank Zappa, Neil Gaiman, and Connie Dobbs. She lives on the Internet at www.grimagix.com, www.dreams overzero.com, and www.reverendvariable.com. In meatspace, she can often be found reading Tarot cards in the quieter taverns and cafes of Portland, Oregon. She frequently has to remind herself to use the Oxford comma.*

Illustrator: Christa Marquez

Witchcraft Essentials

PRACTICES, RITUALS & SPELLS

Making Time for Magick

Melanie Marquis

Ah, balance! It's difficult to define or maintain, yet we strive to understand it and achieve it nonetheless. Imbalance, on the other hand, seems to follow us around whether we want it or not. When life gets hectic, it's all too easy for our priorities to shift out of equilibrium and the big picture to sway out of focus. We get caught up in the details of the hour and we forget to enjoy the moments. This never-stop, never-get-it-all-done routine can wear a person down fast, and it will sap your strength that could otherwise be used for good magick.

Whether you work, go to school, take care of kids, or take care of yourself, there's not always enough time in the day to take care of a full list of obligations. We fall behind on our responsibilities, and our energy levels wane in response. The pressure to achieve the impossible—i.e., a balanced lifestyle where you're on top of the world and the laundry, too—can make even the most powerful Witches feel overwhelmed and ineffective.

Magick is your ace in the hole here. While it might seem counterintuitive to assume that taking more time for magick will actually create more time, that's exactly what happens when we bump ritual and spellwork to the top of our to-do list. When we're in the circle, when we're working a spell, when we're in touch with the gods and the goddesses, time stands still, if it stands at all. We enter a space that exists beyond time, beyond restriction. It's a sacred place, and in that place we can create more of what we want and need, be it resources, luck, or a few more minutes to take care of the day's obligations. That's just one side of it, though. Making more time for magick has two components: literally making more time, magickally, as just mentioned, and also finding more ways to work a little magick into our everyday routines and responsibilities. Here are a few fun and easy ways to do both.

Magick to Make More Time

If you'd like to do some spellwork to create at least the illusion of more time, you have a few different options. One way to go is to focus the magick on speeding through tasks that ordinarily seem to take forever. To accomplish this aim, you might try a bit of imitative charmwork. If you want to speed up washing the dishes, for example, you might begin by casting a circle around your sink to transform it into a sacred space for magick. Fill the sink with water, then sprinkle in just a touch of peppermint oil to impart a brisk, quick-moving energy. Then wash or mock-wash the dishes at a frenzied hyper-speed, taking much less time than usual to complete (or fake-complete) the task. State your intention in no uncertain terms: "I wash dishes very quickly; it takes hardly any time at all!" you might chant to yourself while you clean. When the dishes and your spell are finished, drain the sink with a final "Quickly, quickly, dishes are cleaned! Quickly, quickly, so mote it be!" You might do this routine with each brand-new dish sponge you break out, letting it soak up the magick in the sink so that it will wash quickly ever on.

Of course, washing dishes is just one not-so-glamorous task you might want to hurry up a bit. If you instead want to speed up the time it takes you to do more professional, less menial work, you might choose to do another sort of spell that also makes use of imitative actions. For instance, you might begin by bringing to your ritual space something that represents your job. If you're a teacher, for example, a piece of chalk or a textbook would suffice; if you're a waiter, bring an apron or a serving tray. A work uniform, any specialized tools of the trade you regularly use, or even a piece of paper with a written description of the work you do each day are all fitting possibilities.

Also take with you into your ritual space a clock with a hand you can adjust. Begin by setting the clock to the time your work day typically starts. Then imitate yourself doing your work while at the same time rapidly turning the dial of the clock to the time when your work shift usually ends. If you don't keep

a regular schedule, just choose a time frame that seems about right, based on the number of hours you tend to work consecutively. As you move the hands on the clock, chant something like, "My work is done; the hours fly!" If possible, bring this magickal clock to work with you; its charmed energy will make the hours spent in drudgery or under pressure seem a little briefer. By making the unpleasant parts of the day move more quickly, you'll feel like you have more time for other, more pleasant things.

By making the unpleasant parts of the day move more quickly, you'll feel like you have more time for other, more pleasant things.

Making more time doesn't always involve speeding stuff up. Another route you might take is to aim for magickally slowing down the time you spend doing the things you really enjoy. The enjoyable hours seem to last much longer, and because of this, the non-enjoyable hours seem to shrink and be less consequential and meaningful, thus creating the illusion of more time.

One way to magickally lengthen the time spent doing enjoyable things is to engage in these activities while in a sacred space, be it physical or mental. If you're an artist, you might cast a magick circle around your studio before you paint your lovely masterpieces. If spending time with a grandchild is the thing you adore, get into a magickal mental state beforehand, letting go of tension, negativity, and anything else that inhibits the feelings of connection, awareness, and compassion that accompany a magickal mindset. Cherish each moment you have to do what you love, whether in the circle or outside of it. By enjoying to the fullest each and every drop of goodness in our blessings, those moments spent in happiness become timeless, magickal—and time itself seems to expand in response.

Time to Make More Magick

Magickally making more time isn't the only game in town. Finding time to make more magick is another way to bring a mystical touch to your everyday life. One approach is to turn mundane activities you have to do anyway into opportunities for ritual and spellwork. If you have a lot of housework to do, for instance, take advantage of the time and make it magickal. Charm your broom and sweep in a spiral pattern to attract desired energies; clean your windows with a cheering potion to bring joy to everyone who enters. If cooking is your thing, choose ingredients with magickal intent in mind, and weave a spell while you prepare the meal.

Stuck in the office all day? Charm your computer keyboard or pen with an energy to keep you sharp and alert, or wear a special piece of jewelry empowered to make your talents shine at the work place. Are there unpleasant personalities in your work environment that you'd rather keep at a distance? You might try secretly casting a magick circle around your desk, office, or cubicle to help repel them from your personal workspace. Do you work a very difficult job that involves hard physical labor? Charm your shoes with a strengthening energy, and empower your socks with a soothing energy; the combination will help you get through the day a little easier.

Whatever job you work—even if you work for yourself—take full advantage of break times. Go outside, if possible, and touch the earth. Enjoy the sight or smell of any nearby vegetation, and ask the earthly elements to recharge you. Feel the power of the sunlight or moonlight; sense the essence of the plants and dirt surrounding you. Soak up the extra energy, and let it give you a boost of power to last through the rest of your work shift.

These simple little charms can go a long way in making your day more enjoyable. Sure, casting a spell on a busy subway train, for instance, is a far cry from casting a spell at your own well-designed, carefully planned altar, but magick is magick, any way you cut it and anywhere you cast it. By bringing magick to the mundane instead of regulating it to only occur under the most optimal conditions, we

 strengthen our connection to the mystical side of things, and we get better at utilizing this connection, too, regardless of the circumstances.

We Witches *need* our magick. Without it, our spirits atrophy. Instead of battling against the clock like it's your sworn enemy, embrace the illusion of time and learn to work it to your advantage by using magick. Sure, we're not actually creating more time, but this simple shift in perspective can make it seem as if we can. You've got some good ideas now of where to begin. Seek out ways to make time for more magick, and design new methods of using magick to artificially create more time. You'll find yourself enjoying more and more magickal moments, and these precious times, as elusive as they are, are what life as a Witch is all about.

Melanie Marquis *is the author of* The Witch's Bag of Tricks (Llewellyn, *2011) and* A Witch's World of Magick (Llewellyn, *2014). She's the founder of United Witches global coven and also serves as local coordinator for Denver Pagan Pride. She's written for many Pagan publications, including* Circle Magazine, Pentacle Magazine, *and* Spellcraft, *and she's a regular contributor to Llewellyn's popular annuals. A freelance writer, folk artist, Tarot reader, nature lover, mother, and eclectic Witch, she's passionate about finding the mystical in the mundane through personalized magick and practical spirituality. Visit Melanie at www.facebook.com/melaniemarquisauthor or www.melaniemarquis.com or on Twitter @unitedwitches.*

Illustrator: Kathleen Edwards

Her Vessels: Chalices, Bowls & Cauldrons

Elizabeth Barrette

A typical set of Pagan altar tools includes a pentacle, a wand, an athame, and a chalice. These represent different aspects of the Divine. Each of them can take on different forms to refine the meaning further. These physical objects help give shape to a ritual, spell, or other activity dealing with subtle forces.

A chalice represents the divine feminine, the Goddess. This tool can also take the form of a bowl or a cauldron. All of these forms share the same basic concept of a cup, a container. That which receives or holds is said to have feminine energy; that which enters or lies within is said to have masculine energy. Much of what practitioners accomplish in ritual comes from combing these two forces in symbolic ways, or otherwise working with the energies represented in the tools. Therefore, it helps to understand exactly what each tool stands for, and how its shape and material can contribute to the overall working.

Shape and Symbolism

All containers share the feminine aspect, but they express it in subtly different ways. Their shape influences their role in ritual use. Consider the three types discussed in this article.

The chalice is the most common form chosen for a Pagan altar: a cup standing above a foot. This represents the interactive feminine by means of a female cup conjoined with a male stem. The chalice embodies the element of water and the western quarter. It is often used with an athame to enact the Great Rite. Practitioners may pass it around the circle when serving cakes and ale, or use it to pour a libation to the gods. It corresponds to the Holy Grail from Arthurian legend. In Tarot, the suit of Cups deals with emotions, both positive and negative.

Chalices are often decorated. They may be etched, engraved, or enameled with patterns. Sometimes they have jewels embedded in the outside. Certain chalices have a sculpted shape, such as a dragon, formed into a cup. They can be among the most ornate of altar tools. Decorations make a chalice stronger in the area(s) corresponding to the chosen symbols, but a plain chalice is more versatile.

The bowl is the simplest of tools, a cup shape by itself. It is typically small, for individual use, and thus represents the personal feminine. A wide, shallow bowl suggests breadth and diversity, while a deep, narrow bowl implies focus and concentration.

Bowls serve a variety of purposes on the altar. They may contain liquids, such as water or oil, or solids, such as salt, earth, or nuggets of incense. A dark, reflective bowl offers an opportunity for scrying. Bowls often come in sets, each one colored or decorated differently to indicate its role. For example, there are pairs of God/Goddess bowls and sets of four or five bowls to represent the elements and directions. Nested sets provide bowls of several sizes that fit inside each other for easy storage. Having multiple bowls on an altar makes it easier to set up everything in advance by sorting the necessary materials each into its own bowl.

The cauldron is a big pot, usually made of metal. It often has feet to stand above the surface it rests upon, or hangers to suspend it in midair, and it may have a lid as well. It serves to hold greater quantities of material and symbolizes the womb of the Goddess. Because of its large size, the cauldron is the coven equivalent of a chalice or bowl.

GUNDESTRUP CAULDRON

Therefore it represents the collective feminine. It embodies the sub-conscious, intuitive, and psychic aspects of personality—that which is hidden in life. It corresponds to the Cauldron of Carridwen, conveying death and rebirth, and the gift of tongues. A famous historical example is the Gundestrup Cauldron, with its mythical figures, although modern cauldrons are usually plain.

Like bowls, cauldrons serve many purposes in ritual. They may hold offerings to the gods or items to be charged. Sturdy ones can be used for cooking, brewing potions, or dipping candles. If properly insulated—one reason they often have feet—they can hold sacred fires, incense, burning candles or spell papers, and so forth. A dark cauldron serves as a jumbo scrying bowl.

Material and Meaning

Magical tools benefit from high quality, because lesser items wear out faster under mystical use. The material used affects not just the lifespan of the tool but also what it can be used to accomplish. Different materials correspond to different elements, deities, and magical purposes. Consider the following factors when selecting your chalice, bowl, or cauldron.

Glass and ceramic are the most inert materials. They typically don't react with their contents or absorb anything, although some types of ceramic glaze are less secure than others. Glass is formed from sand (earth) and fire, so it has the strongest connection to those elements; but it can also be clear, like water and air, so it has secondary connections there. Ceramic embodies a balance among all four elements, which makes it suitable for any purpose.

These two materials take color more easily than others used to make chalices, bowls, and cauldrons. Having tools of different colors is a great way to distinguish their purposes. White or clear may be used for anything, but especially for purification. Red conveys love, passion, and courage; it often appears in linked handfasting chalices or items for women's mysteries. Orange relates to success, progress, and celebration. Yellow deals with cheerfulness and communication. Green brings fertility, prosperity, and healing. Blue corresponds to calm, wisdom, and dreams. Many containers are blue, due to the strong connection with the element of water. Violet relates to psychic ability and higher powers. Black deals with meditation, divination, banishing, and protection. Scrying bowls are usually black. A pair of black and white chalices may represent the Goddess and the God.

Chalices are frequently made from glass or ceramic. These can be quite delicate, especially those of blown glass; but sturdier ones from cast or pressed glass also exist. Glass bowls are less common. Ceramic is a popular material for bowls. Those made on a potter's wheel capture the spiral motion in their energy signature, and may retain a spiral pattern in the bottom, which is another feminine symbol. Cauldrons are rarely made from glass or ceramic.

Wood corresponds to the element of earth, although in the Eastern tradition it's an element in its own right. Wood is reactive and absorptive, although it can be sealed; it's best for containing solid rather than liquid things. It has the advantage of being easy to carve. For people who like to make their own tools, wood is a good choice; other materials typically require more specialized equipment to work. Wooden bowls are common, wooden chalices less so, and wooden cauldrons rare.

Each type of wood possesses its own magical qualities. Apple brings feminine energy, fertility, peace, and abundance; it is the wood of the ban-draoi, or woman-druids. Ash is the world tree, and can represent that when carved into a stemmed chalice. Birch, another feminine wood, also conveys cleansing and rebirth; it's ideal for water blessings. Bloodwood has a deep reddish-purple color that suits it for women's mysteries. Ebony is dark, almost black, and is ideal for scrying bowls. Hazel conveys magic and wisdom,

CHALICES

CERAMIC

GLASS

WOOD

METAL

particularly when carved with the salmon of knowledge. Maple balances feminine and masculine energies; this common wood aids

travel, knowledge, and creativity. Oak is a masculine wood, useful for balancing gender polarity by making it into a feminine shape. Willow has strong feminine and lunar connections, and also enhances healing magic; it is a popular choice for medicine bowls. Yew has a bright yellow hue, good for

communication, but it also has martial connotations because it's used to make longbows.

Metal corresponds to the element of earth, although in Eastern traditions it also is an element of its own. It is nonabsorptive, although it will react with some substances, especially acidic ones. It is also the most durable material used for containers. Metal is the most popular material for cauldrons, and also appears in bowls and chalices. Some chalices have a metal stem with a glass cup, allowing for the combination of different energies.

The type of metal affects the magical qualities inherent in the container. Brass relates to the sun, fire, and masculine energy, and is good for prosperity and protection. It's a cheap, plentiful substitute for gold, which is usually unavailable and also too soft for more than plating. Brass makes excellent bowls and is occasionally used for cauldrons or chalices. Copper connects with Venus, water, and feminine energy, and is ideal for love, healing, and luck. Copper is one of the best materials for containers, and is popular for cauldrons and occasionally used for bowls. Iron deals with Mars, fire, and masculine energy, and is good for protection, grounding, shielding, and martial uses. Cast iron is by far the most common material for cauldrons, and stainless steel chalices are also available. Silver matches the moon, water, and feminine energy; it can absorb all kinds of magical influences. Among its many applications are communication, dreams, healing, love, peace, protection, and psychic ability. Because silver is soft and expensive, most such containers consist of silver alloy or silver plate over another metal. Silver bowls and chalices are more common than cauldrons.

Stone is an uncommon material, because it's more challenging to carve and often more expensive. However, it enables the use of stone magic in combination with altar tools. Chalices and bowls are occasionally made from stone. Alabaster is a soft white stone that conveys purity and protection, and is historically used for chalices, bowls, and other containers. Carnelian comes in orange to red and connects with fire, courage, and strength. Hematite is silver-black for grounding and banishing. Jade comes in many earth colors, most famously green; it brings healing, longevity, and prosperity. Lapis is deep blue and is suited for water magic and psychic work. Onyx also comes in different colors and is cheap and easy to carve; it's a good all-purpose stone, while black onyx is favored for scrying tools. Malachite has bands of green and black; it's good for healing and love work. Marble may be white, black, or pink and is easy to carve—another all-purpose stone. Quartz has qualities depending on its color, such as rose quartz for love. An amethyst chalice is said to prevent drunkenness and poisoning. Quartz bowls may be tapped or rubbed to create musical tones, and are ideal for air magic. Soapstone is cheap and easy to carve, and is good for grounding and balancing.

Choosing Vessels

With so many options, it can be confusing to figure out what you need. First, consider the size. If you're a solitary practitioner, you probably need just a chalice or a small bowl. If you belong to a coven, it helps to have a chalice and a set of several bowls, and possibly a small cauldron. If you host events with a bunch of people, then try to find a good-sized cauldron and a larger chalice, so that people can see the objects from a distance.

Also think about what you do. If you only have one little altar table, you don't need a lot of equipment. If you set up individual altars at each quarter, then you'll need more, which goes back to the fact that bowls often come in sets and chalices may be tinted to suggest different elements. If you like to brew things or combine things, you'll need a cauldron for that. Scrying in this context requires a dark bowl or cauldron.

Remember that materials and decorations influence the effectiveness. If you only want to have one or two items, choose plain ones so you can use them for anything. However, if you do a lot of work in a particular field of magic, it helps to have specialized tools for that. A love worker might want a red glass chalice or a copper cauldron. A healer might prefer a ceramic chalice decorated with gods of health and a set of small bowls carved from malachite and jade.

Shop or craft thoughtfully. Take your time to find vessels that really suit your needs; don't just grab the first thing you see. Your magical tools leave an impression on everything you do with them. Make sure they're the right ones.

Elizabeth Barrette's *full bio appears on page 44.*

Illustrator: Rik Olson

Five Essential Stones
for Witches

Deborah Blake

Earth, air, fire, and water—these are the elements around which we build a Witchcraft practice. Many of us are drawn more strongly to one element than to another, but we tend to call on, interact with, and depend on them all. So it is a good idea to have tools that help you to connect with each element. In the case of earth, I highly recommend five essential stones as part of the well-rounded Witch's toolkit.

I will confess to a great affection for stones in general, perhaps because I am a Taurus and therefore an earth sign. Or maybe because I just like shiny things that fit nicely in the hand and have a certain significant heft to them. I like all kinds: tumbled stones that the ocean throws out of her watery depths to lay upon the beach, glittering faceted crystals cut out of the side of a mountain, red ones, blue ones, and even plain old brown ones. It is probably no accident that I ended up as a jewelry maker, among other things, crafting beautiful adornments out of gemstones of many varied hues and shapes.

The Stones

As a Witch, I have five stones in particular that I have come to rely on. All of them are fabulous to look at, but they are also among the most powerful and functional of all the gemstones used in magick today. If you are only going to have a few stones in your collection, I suggest you start with these.

AMETHYST

Amethyst's powers are spiritual, emotional, psychic, and physical; there isn't much territory this lovely purple stone doesn't cover. In the spiritual realm, amethyst is known for granting peace and aiding in meditation, and is useful for those fighting addiction. It helps with insomnia, is a de-stressor, and can help lend courage to one who carries it. It may be best known for its ability to help boost psychic ability, however. Tuck it under your pillow for prophetic dreams, or place a chunk on your altar when seeking answers. I like to keep a small amethyst crystal tucked into the bag that holds my Tarot cards; it protects, cleanses, and empowers them, all at the same time. Amethyst is one of the stones associated most strongly with love, and is used in magick for both finding and sustaining loving relationships. In fact, it is one of the few stones that is good for helping with general happiness, lifting the spirits and promoting clear thinking. It is also a strongly protective stone, and is used for safety while traveling, against thieves and accidents, and to ward off illness. Amethyst can be used for healing, especially when the issue is emotional or psychological in nature rather than physical (although it works for that, too). Because of its purple color, it is sometimes used for crown chakra work.

CRYSTAL QUARTZ

Crystal quartz is a general power-boosting crystal, especially when used under the full moon, since it is associated with the Goddess.

Many magick users place quartz crystals on the top of wands or staffs, or keep a large cut crystal on their altars. (I have one myself. Or possibly six or seven. You can't have too many quartz crystals, since different sizes and shapes lend themselves to different uses.) Crystal quartz is a powerful tool when used in healing work. Stones can be placed on areas where the body's energy is blocked, or used to absorb negative energy from people or spaces. Crystal quartz is another psychic booster as well, and can be placed under a pillow or in with Tarot cards or rune stones to aid in clear vision. The "crystal ball" used by psychics was originally made from crystal quartz, although these days, alas, such things are difficult to find (not to mention expensive). However, a cut crystal will work just as well; sometimes the tiny flaws and imperfections will actually help by forming shapes and images to guide the viewer. Crystal quartz is powerfully protective, and a good stone to have with you in circle if you are doing any form of magickal work where you feel particularly vulnerable. If you don't want to invest in a large crystal, you can purchase a strand of quartz chips and place them around your sacred space. Be aware that quartz comes in many different colors and variations (rose quartz, smoky quartz, and so on), but they each have particular strengths and cannot necessarily be used interchangeably. If you can have only one stone, crystal quartz is the one I recommend for all Witches.

LAPIS

Lapis lazuli, to give it its full name, has long been associated with queens and goddesses. This blue stone, most commonly seen as royal blue but also found in variations that range from denim color to navy, is sometimes flecked with pyrite, which looks like bits of gold. Little wonder the ancient Egyptians valued it so much. Lapis, like most other blue stones, is strongly associated with healing. It also brings calm and peace, promotes love and joy, and lends courage to those who wear it. Lapis is a protective stone as well, and is said to have a positive effect on concentration and mood. Because of its healing nature and its affinity for love and happiness, this stone is a particularly good one to carry or place on your altar if you struggle with health issues or depression (as an adjunct to proper medical care, of course).

MOONSTONE

Moonstone is probably the gemstone most closely associated with the Goddess. It is, after all, the stone of the moon. Usually a milky white or creamy off-white, moonstone also can be found as my particular favorite, rainbow moonstone, which carries within it a special iridescent, opal-like gleam. Because of its close ties to the Goddess and the moon, moonstone is often used for wands, staffs, and ritual jewelry. As befits a stone dedicated to the Goddess, moonstone is known for its strength in both drawing and nurturing love, as well as protection magick and increasing psychic ability. I have found moonstone to be a gentle stone, working in more subtle and quiet ways, unlike the sometimes overwhelming power of amethyst and crystal quartz. If you find that you are a little too sensitive to many forms of magick, then moonstone may be the perfect stone for you.

TURQUOISE

Turquoise has been prized by cultures the world over, from the Chinese to the Native Americans of the Unites States. It is another all-around powerful stone, used primarily for protection (especially in conjunction with black onyx, another strongly protective stone), healing, and love. Turquoise can bring courage and good fortune, and is an excellent stone to use in prosperity work as well. Turquoise can vary from bright blue, to a softer blue-green, to green-brown.

The most prized turquoise, a vivid robin's-egg blue, comes from only one place, the Sleeping Beauty mine in Arizona. But turquoise doesn't have to be expensive or perfect-looking to be powerful. As with other stones, how a piece of turquoise looks is less important than how it feels. (Do be careful, however, that you are getting real turquoise—because of its expense and the over-working of mines, more and more people are starting to substitute look-alike stones for turquoise. Be wary if something seems unusually cheap.)

Choosing a Stone

That brings us to the next important facet (please excuse the pun) of using gemstones in magickal work: choosing the stone that is perfect for you. All stones are *not* created equal. In fact, many people believe that stones vibrate at different frequencies or have their own particular energy. They may not be alive in the way that we think of life, but they are a chunk of Earth, and as such, can vary widely, especially the larger pieces. If you intend to use a stone for magickal work (as opposed to a merely decorative purpose), you may want to take some time picking out just the right stone.

If you order a crystal over the Internet, as many of us have on oc-

casion, you just have to hope that the right one finds its way to you. But if you are fortunate enough to be able to choose from among a variety of specimens at a store or craft show, I highly recommend taking the time to pick up each rock that appeals to you. Hold each one in your hands, close your eyes, and

shut out the rest of the world as much as possible. Try to feel if there is a connection there, something that says "yes, this one" or else "no, not this one." I once spent two hours in a New Age shop looking for just the right rose quartz crystal during a time when I was in particular need of calm and peace. It was well worth it to end up with a stone that worked for me.

Sometimes a stone just calls to you. One of the lessons of a Witchcraft practice is learning to be open to the messages of the universe and the world around us. I have a beautiful chunk of lapis that practically ordered me to take it home; I realized it was meant to be mine when I didn't want to put it back down on the table where it had been displayed. I couldn't afford it, and I hadn't intended to buy another stone, but there it was, clutched in my hand as though it were the last, best rock in the world. Needless to say, it is sitting on my altar right this very minute. It has been a powerful adjunct to my energy healing work, so apparently it really was supposed to come home with me.

Whether you are out searching for the perfect stone to use in your magickal practice, or just happen to pass one in a window display that catches your eye and won't let go, be open for the stone that is a good match for your energy and your needs.

Caring for Your Stones

You may not think of pieces of rock as needing any particular care, but if you intend to use them as part of your magickal and spiritual toolkit, you will want to do a little more than toss them in a bowl and let them gather dust. Neglect won't necessarily hurt the stone (the way silver would tarnish or an herb would wither and die without water), but like any other magickal tool, your stones should be treated with respect. Remember that they represent the element of earth, and it isn't a good idea to take an element for granted!

If you have a special place for your magickal tools, you may wish to store your stones there. I bought a beautiful glass-front wooden cabinet (locally made, out of reclaimed woods, by an artist I knew—all bonuses, energetically speaking) that I use to house many of my crystals and magickal oils and my sage wand (so Magic the Cat doesn't eat it). The clear front is especially nice because the stones are still visible—and therefore I remember to use them—but they are kept safe from stray energy I might not want on them.

If, like me, you always have at least a few stones out on your altar (or altars), be sure to clean them occasionally. Make sure they are not dusty or dirty, and if you use them for healing or magickal work on a regular basis, you may wish to cleanse them periodically by leaving them out in the moonlight on the night of the full moon, or by rinsing them in running water or in a bath of sea salt and water. Watch your stones for signs that they have absorbed negative energy and need to be cleaned; this usually shows up as a darkening of any lines or shadows within the stone.

Whether your magickal stones are in the form of faceted cut crystals or tumbled rocks, or even set into jewelry, these gifts from the earth can be a powerful and beautiful part of your Witchcraft practice. One (or all) of these five stones is sure to add an extra boost to your magickal work and to your life in general.

. . . .

For more information on working with stones, I highly recommend Scott Cunningham's book *Cunningham's Encyclopedia of Crystal, Gem & Metal Magic* (Llewellyn, 2002).

Deborah Blake *is the author of* Everyday Witch Book of Rituals; Circle, Coven and Grove; Everyday Witch A to Z; The Goddess Is in the Details; Everyday Witch A to Z Spellbook; *and the* COVR Award–winning Witchcraft on a Shoestring, *all from Llewellyn. She has published numerous articles in Pagan publications, including Llewellyn annuals, and has an ongoing column in* Witches & Pagans Magazine. *Her award-winning short story "Dead and (Mostly) Gone" is included in the* Pagan Anthology of Short Fiction: 13 Prize Winning Tales *(Llewellyn, 2008). Deborah has been interviewed on television, radio, and podcast, and can be found online at Facebook, Twitter, and http://deborahblake.blogspot.com. When not writing, Deborah runs the Artisans' Guild, a cooperative shop she founded with a friend in 1999, and also works as a jewelry maker. She lives in a hundred-year-old farmhouse in rural upstate New York with five cats who supervise all her activities, both magickal and mundane.*

Illustrator: Jennifer Hewitson

Solitude & Quiet: Important Tools for the Magickal Practitioner

Susan Pesznecker

Something extraordinary is happening in the world today. We're undergoing a paradigm shift: a fundamental change in the way our culture and world community function as well as in what we value and believe to be important. The idea is nothing new—these shifts have happened throughout recorded human history. The difference? In past centuries, we've only recognized paradigm shifts when we looked back after a hundred or more years and realized that the Renaissance or Iron Age or Roman Empire or Age of Enlightenment had changed everything. But today? This is the first time we've been swept up in a paradigm shift while simultaneously being aware it's happening.

What's the current fundamental shift? Why, the digital revolution, of course. Most of us today live lives deeply entwined with and organized by digital technology. Whether using a laptop, smart phone, or tablet, we've come to depend on these tools as critical to our everyday lives and routines. In addition to the rapid influx of technology into our daily lives, the Internet itself has proven a particularly wonderful boon to the Pagan community, allowing us to network, teach, share information, and form community in ways impossible before. It's a fascinating time, and it's neither fad nor temporary: the changes are happening from one day to the next, and experts point to the ways our lives are rapidly being changed. For a fascinating view into this transformation, search the Web for a video called "Social Revolution 2," and fasten your seat belt.

So, here we are—inhabiting a world in which much of the daily routine has become "simplified" by the digital revolution. I use my tablet and laptop to teach, talk with friends, manage a Druid Order, make art, follow the news, read books, pay bills, find recipes, take photos, manage e-mails, play games, watch movies, track the natural world, level the stones placed in my backyard labyrinth, stargaze, and more. The world is, quite literally, at my fingertips.

But at what cost?

Evidence is pouring in that the current epidemic of obesity, reduced fitness, and increases in chronic disease are due at least in part to the explosion of technology. We're sitting too much: many of our (increasingly tech-oriented) jobs are sedentary, and then we come home, tired, and sit some more. A number of studies show a direct relationship between sitting more than six hours per day and a dramatic increase in sudden death. Weak bones and vitamin D deficiency are reaching epidemic levels in adults and children, a direct result of our failure to spend time outdoors and to keep moving. Vitamin D is created when sun hits the skin, and we're not getting enough. There's also rising evidence that much of the ADD/ADHD epidemic may be traceable to a syndrome being called Nature Deficit Disorder, which results when our addiction to technology effectively separates us from the natural world and the outdoors. These are only some of the scarier potential effects of the digital age on our health, and it's clear we're going to have to make some adjustments, a detailed exploration of which is beyond the scope of this short essay.

There's more. Many in the Pagan community are increasingly concerned about how the digital lifestyle is altering Pagan community and, in many cases, pulling people away from face-to-face interaction in favor of tweets and Facebook groups. We all know people who seemingly spend hours a day in front of screens, responding instantly—at any time of the day or night—to e-mails, Facebook messages, etc. Yet many of them have slowed or stopped their participation in face-to-face (f2f) Pagan community. At a recent inservice on my college campus, the speaker told us that many people today—especially those under thirty—are "heavy users" of technology, meaning they may spend ten or more hours each day engaging with screens. At the same time, they spend little time with f2f people—or, if they're hanging out with f2f people, they often ignore them, preferring discourse and interaction with their smart phones over the flesh-and-blood humans

Many in the Pagan community are increasingly concerned about how the digital lifestyle is altering Pagan community and, in many cases, pulling people away from face-to-face interaction in favor of tweets and Facebook groups.

sitting next to them. Many people today say they prefer texting over phoning people or speaking directly to them.

To be fair, many will argue that cyberspace is every bit as important and valuable as is the f2f world (sometimes called "meatspace," a term I intensely dislike and do not use). Digital space has specific advantages: for some Pagans, electronic connection may be their only way to interact with like-minded people, and there's no doubt that social media has expanded all of our horizons in terms of communication. I've "met"—in cyber rather than f2f terms—people in different states or countries whom I'd never have gotten to know if it weren't for Facebook or other social media, and this has enriched my world. Yet I wonder if the ease of cyber communication is coming at the expense of f2f relationships. Is it so easy to be present online that Pagans are choosing to be less active in real-space groups?

Will there be a cost for these choices? For a spiritual tradition that has worked for decades to increase public acceptance, visibility, etc., is the Pagan migration to the Web undermining those efforts? Or will it prove to be a positive phenomenon, forging new—albeit different—bonds and making our community even stronger?

This brings us to another critical consideration. Most of us in the Pagan community are practitioners of magick in some guise. Whether our magick is simple and nature-based or highly ritualized and ceremonial, whether we call the quarters or invoke the three realms, or whether we invite patrons or invoke daemons, we work with the energies and forces collectively known as "magick," and this requires its own skill set. We manage energy through grounding, centering, meditation, or other practices. We contemplate purpose and muster intention. We borrow or pull down energy from external sources, using it to infuse and accomplish our magickal goals. And perhaps most importantly, the act of magick requires us to leave the space of the everyday and enter the realm of the sacred, stepping out of the familiar and into the space of the "other."

Can these actions be accomplished through the digital realm?

Many will say, "Yes, of course." And they may be at least partially right. It is possible to conduct rituals and meetings online via video conferencing, send Reiki energy through the ether, and erect cybershrines where people may leave prayers and electronic offerings. It's interesting and, given the reality of the digital age, encouraging that folks are trying to find ways to merge magick and technology. But I'm still concerned, and here's why.

I believe that magick in its most essential nature works from a place of inner silence and inner focus. It begins for us humans as a spark—an internal cynosure that gathers our attention. Sometimes we create this focus, but other times it happens around us—as an alerting action. In either case, we must be alert, observant, and quiet

enough to notice and respond to the energy and the changes that ensue. But with the uber-presence of the Internet—our eyes fixed on a screen, our ears plugged with MP3 ear-buds, and our fingers tap-tap-tapping away at a keyboard—I fear we're often too distracted to notice. The near-constant digital sensory bombardment makes it impossible to be silent within ourselves, to understand silence, work in solitude—internal or external—and use the powers of silence and solitude to work for us and our magickal purposes. Simply said, when the world is too noisy, the wee inner voice is easily overwhelmed. Even more worrisome, we seem to be forgetting how valuable and important silence can be, how very *essential* it is to us as magickal people. These behavioral changes are, without a doubt, affecting our spiritual lives.

Concepts of silence and solitude tie in closely to the practice of intention. Many of us practice magick on a daily basis, but all too often the practice becomes routine—tossed off—or is done without a necessary depth of thought. Without internal silence, it's almost impossible to develop intention or a state of mindfulness—i.e., a calm, watchful, focused awareness of internal and external conditions, consciousness, and perceptions. These processes are active rather than passive: a mindful worker of magick engages actively with them and, through this, hopes to be successful or even reach a new point of enlightenment. This requires silence, both inner and outer, and it may also require periods of solitude, sans distractions.

In these ways, the digital world works against us. It's not unusual for people today to try to do several tasks at once, and most of us think we're pretty good at this, believing ourselves to be successful multitaskers. But we're wrong. Recent studies show that when we think we're multitasking, we're actually carrying out rapid serial tasking, our brains hastily shifting from one task to another (Ophir et al.). In truth, this actually slows us down, makes our actions less efficient, and has a profoundly disorganizing effect on the brain. Multitasking causes us to do a worse job at individual activities and leaves us much less likely to retain a sound memory of each activity or its results. It's also exhausting. Further, a frantically busy, scattered mind that jumps rapidly from one place to the next cannot find silence and will be even more challenged to be mindful or to develop focused, concentrated intention.

If we accept that humans require solitude, quiet, and peace in order to give our brains a chance to pant a little and catch up, in order

to be quiet within ourselves, in order to reach that place from which intention and magick spring... how can we get better at this?

Simple: Slow down. Disconnect. Embrace silence.

Here are some suggestions:

- Step away from electronics for at least a few hours each day. Better yet, have a digital-free day each week. Read a book, go for a walk, make some art, step into the garden, or, in whatever way is pleasing to you, be present in the world. Remain silent, if possible, and as your awareness of quiet builds, focus on sensory awareness—i.e., on how the world around you sounds, looks, feels, tastes, or even smells. Feel the magick that surrounds you.

- If you have work to do, make a list and experience the joyful calm of focusing on one task at a time, giving each activity your full, undivided attention until it's complete and not allowing yourself to be distracted. Unplug from technology as you work and create an environment that's silent externally as well as internally, ensuring you're fully present in the moment.

- Practice honing your powers of observation. Take a walk outside (leave the phone and MP3 player behind) and be aware of the sights and sounds. Each time you venture out, make it a goal to see, hear, or feel something you've never noticed before.

- Have "mindful moments." Select cues to respond to, such as stepping through a specific doorway or seeing the color purple. When the cue happens, pause, take a deep breath, and become mindful; hold this for a few minutes, then take a deep cleansing breath and return to your work.

- When working with magick, set aside enough time to fully experience the activity. Create a quiet, distraction-free setting (turn the smartphone *off*), ground and center, and be fully present in the moment. Give yourself time to silence your inner voice, allowing your internal solitude to provide a foundation for magickal intention. Be mindful and fully aware of each step.

May the blessings of silence be yours.

Sources

Louv, Richard. *Last Child in the Woods: Saving Our Children from Nature-Deficit Disorder.* Chapel Hill, NC: Algonquin Books, 2005. See also the *New York Times* review at www.nytimes.com/2005/04/28/garden/28kids.html.

Ophir, Eyal, Clifford Nass, and Anthony D. Wagner. "Cognitive Control in Media Multitaskers." *Proceedings of the National Academy of Sciences* (July 2009), www.scribd.com/doc/19081547/Cognitive-control-in-media -multitaskers.

Qualman, Erik. "Social Media Revolution 2 (Refresh)." *Vimeo.* 2010. vimeo .com/11551721.

Susan Pesznecker *is a writer, college English teacher, and hearth Pagan/ Druid living in northwestern Oregon. Her magickal roots include Pictish Scot and eastern European/Native American medicine traditions. Sue holds a master's degree in nonfiction writing and loves to read, stargaze, camp with her wonder poodle, and play in her biodynamic garden. She's co-founder of the Druid Grove of Two Coasts and teaches nature studies and herbalism in the online Grey School. Sue has authored* Crafting Magick with Pen and Ink *(Llewellyn, 2009) and* The Magickal Retreat *(Llewellyn, 2012) and regularly contributes to the Llewellyn annuals. Visit her at www.susan pesznecker.com and www.facebook.com/SusanMoonwriterPesznecker.*

Illustrator: Tim Foley

The Art of Dedication

Thuri Calafia

W ell," my friend sarcastically intoned to the air in general, "how dedicated *are* you?" in response to my questioning whether it's timely or fair for her to require Dedicant-level Wicca students to read *The White Goddess.* I must admit she had a point.

Throughout my many years as a Witchcraft teacher, her words have come back to me, time and again, and not just the part about reading requirements.

So just what is dedication, anyway? In an amicable interview with a gentleman who produced a Wild West show in the Midwest a few years ago, I learned that dedication is not at all the same as commitment. In the interview, I'd mentioned that he must be really dedicated in order to pull off such an event single-handedly, as the work involved seemed daunting.

"No," he said, "I'm not dedicated; I'm committed."

"Well, what's the difference?" I asked.

"Imagine yourself sitting down to a good old-fashioned country breakfast," he said. "You've got some eggs, some cream for your coffee,

and a nice thick slice of ham. Now those chickens and cows, well, they're dedicated, because they produce those products every day without fail. And that's a happy thing. But the pig? Now that pig is committed!" He laughed heartily at his own joke.

As a Wicca teacher, I think I trip myself up sometimes when I expect my Dedicant-level students to show the same degree of commitment to their spiritual path that my Initiates typically do. And I'm an eclectic Wiccan—not nearly as strict as more traditional teachers! I must admit that I get frustrated when students blow off class at the last minute to go to the beach or shopping, or when they suddenly drop out of school without a word. I am bewildered and dismayed by the indifference some of them exhibit towards their homework, their promises, and their spiritual path, when those very same students turn around and request, and expect, dedication rituals. I'm usually inclined, at that point, to ask the question my friend did at the beginning of this article, because, as far as I can see, they're thinking of their spiritual path as some sort of ... hobby.

So, okay, dedication isn't commitment. I get that. I also get that the word *commitment* doesn't necessarily enter a student's vocabulary, much less their attitude, until well past the middle of their Dedicant year, if ever. And I understand that a lot of people's attitudes toward their spiritual path seem to be regional—for example, entire communities can be much less serious about their spiritual/magical path than other communities. So, of course, this is going to affect the student's attitude, practices, and seriousness as well. It's clear that some communities' spiritual leaders are more inclined to teach the principles of commitment and dedication than others are. This is something I aspire to, and my students will agree, as the only ones who ever truly "make it" in Circles School are the ones who are capable of both dedication and the resulting commitment that is born of it.

I think another piece of this puzzle is that many, many traditions do not give dedication rites the attention or respect they deserve. After all, someone who is ready to dedicate themselves to study for a year and a day is usually a person who has done a 180-degree turn from the religion of their childhood and culture. So although it's not the huge "graduation" that initiation is, dedication is still a major change in thinking and is indeed a serious step, a big deal. As such, is deserving of much more than the five-minute afterthought tacked on to the end of a coven's regular esbat rite that we usually see.

… although it's not the huge "graduation" that initiation is, dedication is still a major change in thinking and is indeed a serious step, a big deal.

When I've had the pleasure and honor of performing dedication rites, I have always made it a separate event, reserving the evening for the candidate's ritual alone. The evening has some of the elements of an initiation, such as having a ritual bath and period of meditation prior to approaching the Gate blindfolded, complete with a some-what formidable Gatekeeper. However, these rites are designed to gently welcome the candidate into the fold, as it were, so there is no challenge with blade at breast, but rather a concerned questioning about the candidate's certainty regarding this step.

Dedication Ritual

For ease of pronoun use, I present this ritual with the candidate be-ing male, but of course it can be done for female candidates as well. The only difference is when the lines regarding "everything a man (or woman) should aspire to be" are the same gender as the candidate, the following line is "become him/her." If the energy is the opposite, the line reads "embrace him/her." For transgender or intersex people, I use whatever's comfortable and appropriate to the candidate.

Once the candidate is inside the Gate, still blindfolded, I take him by the hand and "spin" him by walking around and around my back yard or other outdoor space until he loses his sense of direc-tion, but again, this is done gently, in a spirit of love and welcome. First, I take him to the east, where an altar is decorated with small tree branches; wands; a besom; spring colors; yellow, pink, and lav-ender candles; feathers; crystals; and other "airy" items.

As he stands there, still blindfolded, I tell him:

This is the domain of the God. His realm encompasses the east, the place
of air, creativity, mental acuity, and logic.

Then helpers come, one by one, and speak softly in his ears:

He is inspiration, morning light, the song of birds. Hear him.
He is all winged creatures, thought, and the sacred seed. Know him.
He is your ability to learn, your eloquence, and your mind. Open to him.

He is the winds of change, the idea in form, the quickening. Let him
  grow in you.
He is the Sacred Muse, truth, and light. He is knowledge. He is every-
  thing a man should aspire to be. Become him.

Then I say:

And now, he belongs to you. Would you see him now, in his glory?

When he says *yes*, I remove his blindfold gently, and let him have a
moment to observe the beauty of the altar before replacing his blindfold and taking him to the middle of the space to spin him again.
Then I take him to the south altar, which is set up with a portable fire
pit, surrounded by lanterns, red sparkly candles, and bright blades lying on a red sparkly cloth.

Again, I address him first:

This is also the domain of the God. His realm encompasses the south, the place of fire, passion, drive, and will.

Again, my helpers come, one by one, and speak softly in his ears:

He is illumination, desire, and protection. Walk always with him.
He is the bright sun, the heat of desire, the creative spark. Let him stir your passion.
He is the blaze of anger that creates a better world, the shaper of dreams. Let him motivate you.
He is the word in motion, action, and aggression. Run with him.
He is the Gentle Savage, the protector, and our sexuality. He is everything a man should aspire to be. Become him.

Then I tell him:

And he now belongs to you. Would you see him now, in his glory?

Again, he is allowed time to observe the altar, and again, the blindfold is replaced, and the candidate is taken to the center, spun, and then taken to the west altar, which is set with a blue satin cloth; a myriad of glass, silver, and crystal goblets and bowls; dozens of shells; strings of faux pearls; silver glitter; and blue, teal, and silver candles.

I say:

This is the domain of the Goddess. Her realm encompasses the west, the place of water, emotions, receptivity, transformation, and submission.

My helpers come and murmur in his ears:

She is the moon which rules the tides, as well as the tides themselves. Let her help you feel the tides within.

> She is the river which fills the lake which leads to the ocean. Flow with
> her.
> She is harmony, peace, and nurturing. Feel her love.
> She is growth. She is the water that sustains life, and she is life itself. Let
> her fill you with her energy.
> She is Maiden, Mother, Crone. She is gentleness, love, and wisdom. She
> is everything a woman should aspire to be. Embrace her.

Again, I say:

> And she now belongs to you. Would you see her now, in her glory?

After the candidate has a moment to observe the beauty of the west altar, he is spun one last time.

For the next step, he is stopped in the middle of the space, and then I tell him:

> You have traveled long now, (candidate), and you have learned many
> things. Some are familiar, and some are new. You know that the
> wisest of all is the Grandmother, the Dark Goddess of birth, death,
> and rebirth. She rules the hidden, the occult—the thing that draws
> so many to this sacred Path. Would you go forth now to the Mystery,
> my friend?

When he says *yes*, his blindfold is removed for the last time, some personal words of praise and encouragement are said regarding the years he has been seeking this path, the trials that have been overcome to get here, and so on. Finally, I go down on one knee to illustrate that in the Art Magical we more senior students (for we are all students) serve our juniors on the path, and I ask:

> Will you do me the honor of allowing me to guide you through to the
> final gate, the gate of the Mystery?

When he says *yes*, I take him by the hand, stop him gently at the gate until I can get through, then beckon to him with open arms. He steps through into my embrace, and then, still holding his hand, I have a helper take his other hand, and together, we pull him along, walking backwards and going down to our knees, pulling him down with us. My other helpers at that point pull and push him into a prone position, on his belly on the ground. We then press him into the ground, stroke his back and arms, and speak to him of the Mystery.

I say:

> This is the domain of the Goddess also. Her realm encompasses the north, the place of earth, the Mystery, the body, manifestation, endings, and beginnings.

My helpers say:

> She is the earth below you. Feel her. Inhale her blessed scent.
> She is the sacred soil which receives his seed and quickens and nurtures new life. Touch her.
> She is the winter, the fallow time, the space between incarnations, and rest. Know her.
> She is midnight, deep roots, history, and our past. Explore her.
> She is the future's promise, the unwritten page, and karma. She is alive and wondrous and fair. Reveal her.
> She is our body, our flesh and our bones. She is the beauty of all that is womankind, and all that a woman should aspire to be. Embrace her.

Then I say:

> And… she is the Mystery! Open to her, and see her now, in her glory.

We turn the candidate over to look at the sky, and I continue:

> *Observe—the Vasty Deep! Out there, other Mysteries, infinite Mysteries of light and dark, of power and promise, of this world and a billion other worlds, unfold and take form. He dances brightly in her dark field, quickening into life, revealing his truth in her love; awakening in all of us the power to change the world!*

Then, I gesture toward the sky, sweeping my arm to indicate the entire universe, and say:

> *And all that she is now belongs to you. Behold—the only thing greater than yourself!*

The ritual continues from this point with the candidate's personal vows regarding study and staying true to himself. Sometimes, if the candidate has requested his measure or a magical name be taken, those actions are also incorporated into the rite.

For cakes and wine, I try to do something that speaks to the element of fire, such as spice cookies or cupcakes, and apple cider or a red wine, mead, or juice. The celebration then continues deep into the night, just as all rites of passage do, with feasting and merriment, congratulations and encouragement, honoring the decision and the future of the Dedicant on his personal path.

Thuri Calafia *is an ordained minister and Wiccan High Priestess, teacher, and founder of Circles School of Wicca and Witchcraft. She is the author of* Dedicant: A Witch's Circle of Fire *and* Initiate: A Witch's Circle of Water, *which are complete courses of study based on her teachings. She is currently working on the third book in the series,* Adept: A Witch's Circle of Earth. *She is actively involved in the Pagan community in the Pacific Northwest, and lives with her beloved partner, Robert, and their four-legged "child," Miss Alyssa Ramone.*

Illustrator: Bri Hermanson

The Three-Circle Possessory Rite

Gede Parma

In my articulation, and in my teaching of possessory phenomena and skill at shifting or deepening consciousness at will, there are two main kinds of possession. The first, which is the most apparent and the most evident in modern Pagan traditions and communities, is Oracular Possession, or what Janet Farrar and Gavin Bone call "Trance Prophesy." This type of possession draws the focus of the gathered human community (for what is possession without human witnesses or tenders?) to the "Seat of the Deity/Spirit" to witness their actions, behavior, and words as in some sense indicative of necessary insights, knowledge, or wisdom to be gained by those assembled. Many times, during Oracular Possession, the vessel will begin physically seated and then begin to prophesy from the Seat. People may choose to approach the deity and ask questions, present concerns, or offer prayers, either as gratitude and in thanks or as something to be fulfilled. The deity may choose to move around the space and to physically interact with those gathered and perform acts of cleansing, banishing, and/or blessing. They may also choose to conjure winds, storms, rains, the sun, or birds, or to cast spells or make magic. Of the two main kinds of possession, these experiences are often more taxing on the vessel carrying the spirit or deity.

The second kind of possession, which the remainder of this essay will examine, can be called "Indulgent Possession." What I mean when I qualify this kind of possession as "indulgent" is that the deity does not incarnate or express through the vessel in order to commit to theatrics or give oracles, but to simply enjoy the pleasures of the flesh—to be manifest among human devotees and celebrants and to indulge in the company. These beings have "bodies" that are not dense like our own, and often "envy" the human experience in many ways. The gods are often fed by the life force given up in sacrifices and offerings that we carefully prepare and reverently offer; however, to be able to taste the food and drink viscerally and immediately is a rare gift. At times this kind of possessory experience may lead to sensual-sexual connections with the gods. Indulgent Possession allows the deities we adore to be among us and within us in such raw and earnest ways that the very offering up of one's body as vessel is offering enough. My community has received a very specific technology that allows us to experience this Indulgent Possession and to offer it in service to and in celebration of our gods. We have developed very particular protocol around this technology and its implementation.

The Three-Circle Possessory Rite (TCPR)

I originally received and crafted this ritual technology in early 2011. Since that time it has been taught and offered up in community many times. The first TCPR was held for Hekate in Brisbane, Queensland, Australia. I received in spontaneous gnosis the concept of three energetically layered (imprinted) and ritually cast circles/rings (not spheres) that would hold the integrity of a rite centered around the possession of celebrants and devotees who wished to merge in holy communion with their beloved deities and to offer the experience of the physically dense and the visceral to these beings who yearn to be with their children and lovers. The following outline of the rite will allow a willing and earnest community of celebrants and devotees to open space and time in which to gather to offer Indulgent Possession with anchoring, revelry, and communion.

Following are the Three Circles of this possessory rite in order of how they are cast and in understanding that they are concentric circles going inward to the center of the space and the altar of offerings:

The First Circle of Witnessing and Rest

The Second Circle of Revelry and Celebration

The Third Circle of Communion and Possession

In this rite, after each of the Circles has been ritually cast and energetically layered into the ground, all begin in the First Circle. All must begin in the Circle of Witnessing and Rest. Then those who are willing to offer evocation or call out to the deity to come and inhabit the Third Circle with the full force of their divine presence walk through the Second Circle to the edge of the Third Circle, and allow the tip of the toes of one foot to touch into the Third Circle to make the invitations. After each call the celebrant returns to the First Circle of Witnessing and Rest.

After the evocations, one or more Priest/esses who have cultivated relationships with the deity to be honored, and ideally are also either lovers or married to the deity, move to the Third Circle to occupy that place as "Center Pole" of the rite for the entire duration of the festivities. The Center Pole is self-possessed and will not become possessed by the deity. There are anchors and tenders (ideally one for every 3–5 people) who act to witness and anchor the rites from the First Circle and do not move from that circle. They also tend those who have returned to the First Circle from the Third Circle of Communion and Possession.

Roles of Leadership (in More Detail)

The roles of leadership required in this rite are as follows:

1. ANCHORS AND TENDERS

Generally speaking, for smaller rites of between 10–20 people, both roles can be fulfilled by the same person. However, in saying that, in this case there needs to be one person as Anchor-Tender for every 3–5 people. If the number of celebrants gathered for the rite surpasses 20, then it is better to have Anchors separate from Tenders, in which case for a group of up to 50 people there could be 4–6 anchors and then 1 tender per 3–5 people (though not all will enter the Third Circle and become possessed). For numbers surpassing 50, it is best to share counsel with community and discuss protocols and the responsibilities of roles.

Anchors and Tenders maintain their presence in the First Circle of Witnessing and Rest throughout the rite. The Anchors are present to keep the energy of the First Circle grounded and clean, and also to an-

chor the energy of all three circles. This is done by grounding into the land directly beneath the place all have gathered within, to maintain a clear and clean energy connection with the earth. An Anchor should ideally be skilled in running energy without imposing anything upon it. It is not the job of the Anchors to "rein in" the rite if it becomes too haphazard or chaotic; that responsibility lies with the Priestess/Center Pole in the Third Circle and the main musical facilitator.

Tenders are individuals who receive those from the Third Circle who may be generally overwhelmed or in need of aid with grounding and returning to a sense of self. Tenders should place vessels of water around the edge of the First Circle, as well as nourishing and grounding foods such as raw fruit and nuts to aid in this process. Generally speaking, the First Circle will be full of cushions and blankets so that the celebrants are comfortable and cared for.

2. Callers

Callers are those who, as explained previously, will layer invitations and evocations to the deity into the Third Circle, praying for the raw, concentrated expression of the deity's potency to occupy the Third Circle. This is essential. Certain deities and spirits have various "epithets," or titles/aspects, and therefore several can be intuitively or consciously chosen for invitation, and then each Caller can focus on a specific aspect of the deity when opening the call.

3. The Center Pole Priest/ess

This Priest/ess, as described previously, has at the very least cultivated a focused and deepened relationship with the deity over several months and feels confident in the art of "spirit/deity negotiation." It is far better if this Center Pole is either married or lover to the deity. The Center Pole also holds the integrity of all three circles and does this by magically becoming the Center Pole, or World Tree, which holds all the worlds/circles together.

Negotiating with a deity in possessory contexts can be a difficult dance. The Center Pole needs to be comfortable with spirit-working in general and on a path of integration, alignment, consciousness, and self-possession. If the rite begins to surpass an appropriate time or if the celebrants who are possessed in the Third Circle seem to be becoming either exhausted or overly unruly, then the Center Pole

Priest/ess can begin to rein the energy back in. This is done with voice, with intent, with will, with confidence, and with authority. I have used something like the following in such situations, but have only done so after feeling intuitively into the edges of the deity and communicating privately my intent:

> *Great Spirit/God/dess, (Name), we, your devotees and celebrants, have gathered here in honor of your presence, power, and possession. We pray now that the tide of your potency recedes, like waves back to the shores of your realms. May the tides recede and may we all be washed in a cleansing water and awaken to our own divine Godhood, which you, and all the Great Ones, aid us in rediscovering and embracing! Hail to (Name) and Bless Your Holy Name!*

The Center Pole walks to the Third Circle after the calls are complete and does not leave the Third Circle until all the celebrants have returned to the First Circle.

4. Musicians

These rites are highly charged and potent occasions that require a matched sense of atmosphere. Musicians are integral to the TCPR. Ideally, there could be many percussion instruments and music makers scattered throughout the Second Circle for those who are revelling to play along with several stationed drummers in the same circle. The most ideal location for the drummers to be playing is on the edge of the third and most central circle. Chants and songs to aid in the dancing and resting upon the rhythms of the drums also add to the intoxication of the event and its participants. It is ideal if there is one main musical facilitator, generally a drummer.

5. GRACES

Another highly integral role is that of the Grace. These individuals, as in Reclaiming Tradition community rituals, are there to keep the harmony flowing within the ritual and to "serve" the assembly gathered in gentle and subtle ways. Within the TCPR, 2–3 Graces (more if there is a gathering of over 40–50 people) may volunteer to move through each circle and into the Third Circle to retrieve food and offerings and serve them to those in the First Circle, and occasionally in the Second Circle. It is ideal that these Graces are trained in the arts of self-possession and in keeping clean and conscious when "sliding" through differing states of consciousness or varying "energy frequencies." Before removing anything from the Third Circle it is polite that the Graces ask those who are in possession to communicate directly with the deity.

Ritual Outline

1. DETERMINE THE DEITY

Before opening space and time to a TCPR, it is necessary to have community consensus on a specific deity. One of the best methods to arrive at a deity for the rite is for all those interested to come together and breathe, ground and center, and align. From this place each person begins to vibrate the names of various deities arising from deep and soulful connection over and over, whether one at a time or several, until the whole group is singing or vibrating one deity's name together. This will happen organically and is not to be forced. If, however, there are several names still being vibrated, the facilitator will call for someone to send a grounding root down into the earth and to witness the vibration of names. The first person to respond that they have sent down the grounding root will begin to deduce the repeated names (usually two or three), and then those particular names will be continuously vibrated by the group until one is arrived at. This is done with ample time before the carrying out of the TCPR, allowing enough time for organization.

2. Organize the Facilitation Team

A group of people volunteer to become essential pieces of the puzzle. A Center Pole priest/ess is required. Anchors, Tenders, Callers, Musicians, and Graces are required. This team holds meetings together to ascertain the time and place of the TCPR, as well to let the community know about the arrangements for the rite. If any volunteers require training in associated skills, then those able to will meet with these individuals and aid in the familiarization of skills of each role. It is ideal for there to be two or three months between determining the deity and the TCPR.

3. (At the Rite) Marking the Boundaries of the Circles and Laying the Offerings

The Center Pole Priest/ess will take on the key facilitation role at the TCPR and will establish, with counsel, the necessary circumference and width of each of the Circles. The gathering celebrants will aid in this process, and all will lay their offerings of food and drink in the middle of the Third/Center Circle with intent and reverence. This is the creation of the altar.

4. Personal Preparation and Alignment

The whole group is led through a grounding and centering and/or alignment to cleanse and clear the intent and the overall energy of the group consciousness.

5. Casting of the Three Circles

The Center Pole Priest/ess will begin the incantations and all will join together. Beginning with the First and most outer Circle, all walk together sun-wise, at least one full circumambulation, and layer the energy into the ground as a ring rather than a sphere.

The First Circle (Outer):

We cast the First Circle, the Circle of Witnessing and Rest—we cast this Circle into the ground, here and now.

The Second Circle (Middle):

We cast the Second Circle, the Circle of Revelry and Celebration—we cast this Circle into the ground, here and now.

The Third Circle (Inner):

> *We cast the Third Circle, the Circle of Communion and Possession—we cast this Circle into the ground, here and now.*

6. THE CALLING OF THE DEITY

All return to the First Circle, and the Priest/ess calls upon those who are offering invitations to the deity. One by one (or all together) the Callers walk to the edge of the Third Circle and may choose to place one foot in that Circle while leaving one in the Second, to speak aloud the evocation. The calls layer over each other and propound the growing concentration of the spirit-force of the deity's presence in the Third Circle.

7. THE CALL TO BEGIN

The Center Pole Priest/ess, self-possessed and grounded, moves to the Third Circle to occupy it completely and calls for the rite to begin.

8. THE MUSICIANS PLAY AND THE CELEBRANTS ENGAGE WITH THE CIRCLES

The music begins and the celebrants, starting in the First Circle, monitor their own experience by choosing when and where to move to the Second Circle of Revelry and Celebration to offer life-force and loosen the fibers, and then whether or not to enter the Third Circle. It is important to note that each person is committed to self-care and not all will choose to enter the Third Circle, or even the Second.

9. Graces Offer Food and Drink to the Possessed/ Deity and the Celebrants of the First Circle

The Graces, like the Anchors and Tenders of the First Circle, retain an anchored grounding root/cord in the earth while moving through the Three Circles. The Graces will walk through the Circles in whichever way they wish, with appropriate mirth and reverence, and from the Third Circle will distribute blessed food and drink offerings to all celebrants, especially those in the First Circle.

10. The Dying Down of the Rite

At some point, not generally pre-established (unless hired space has a time limit), the Center Pole Priest/ess will connect eyes with the main musical facilitator (or vice versa) and the drumming, etc., will be brought to a gradual close.

11. The Call to Prayer

The Priest/ess will now open the circles to prayer, and any and all who wish to come to the edge of the Third Circle and make aloud or silent prayers to the deity may do so. Talismans, charms, jewelry, or whatever may also be consecrated and blessed at this time.

12. Blessings to the Deity

All those who offered invitation and evocation may return to the edge of the Third Circle, individually or all together, and pay homage and give blessings to the deity. The Center Pole Priestess keys into the final "release" of the concentrated presence of the spirit-force and declares the rite complete.

13. The Releasing of the Three Circles

This is done in order from the Third and Inner Circle to the First and Outer Circle. This is done widdershins (against the sun), walking as a group in silence. After each circle is unraveled, the whole group reaches in and "picks up" the substance of the circle and throws it to the farthest direction, saying aloud:

We release this Circle to the Circle of Infinity.

All turn inward, facing each other with hands in prayer position over heart, and repeat the same seal.

14. Deconstruction of Space and Distribution of the Remaining Food and Drink Offerings

Those who have placed personal items in the Center Circle for the altar will now reclaim these possessions, as well as any talismans and/or charms, etc. Remaining food and drink offerings may be distributed among the celebrants or given to the earth, if appropriate. The space is cleaned and cleared and returned to its original, or better, state!

Repeat Step 1 if another TCPR is planned for the near future.

Gede Parma *is a Wild Witch, Pagan Mystic, initiated Priest, and award-winning author. He is an initiate and teacher of the WildWood Tradition of Witchcraft, a hereditary healer and seer with Balinese-Celtic ancestry, and an enthusiastic writer. Gede is a proactive and dynamic teacher and is also the creator and facilitator of the two-year Shamanic Craft Apprenticeship. He teaches both within Australia and internationally. Gede's spiritual path is highly syncretic, fusing a variety of Craft and Mystic traditions. He is also the devoted priest and lover of Aphrodite, Hermes, Hekate, the Blue God, Persephone, and the Sacred Four of the WildWood.*

Illustrator: Christa Marquez

Spellcrafting Essentials:
Those Versatile Components

Raven Digitalis

Witchcraft is an incredibly versatile science and art, and has a variety of interpretations depending on the culture. Some adherents of magick say that true Witchcraft requires no tools whatsoever. While I agree with this statement in the most general sense, I also realize that we humans are intellectual creatures who rely on constant, persistent symbolism throughout our lives. Ingredients, components, and exacting procedures are not necessary to weaving one's intention into the universe, but they can most definitely lend a helping hand.

I remember first getting into the Craft around the age of sixteen. At that time, I was mesmerized by the Hollywood portrayals of the magickal arts, particularly with films like *The Craft* and *Practical Magic*, and, of course, the ever-cheesy-yet-eye-candied series *Charmed*. These programs drew upon true Wiccan and Pagan practices and ideals, yet they "Hollywoodized" them to the extreme. In addition to being entertaining, they were encouraging.

One of the ideas perpetuated in those programs was that spells had to be performed by the book. Therefore, regardless of whether any Craft book told me otherwise, I was determined to perform spells as they were written, from the book, to the letter. I didn't question this notion until I later discovered ancient grimoires that gave extremely complicated directions for simple outcomes: do I really have to circle a poplar tree three times widdershins at midnight on a new moon, spit into the east, say some barbarous names, and recite psalms in order to pick a magickally charged poplar bud for a banishing spell, or can I just go pluck one and say thanks to the tree?

One of my magickal elders once taught me that there's a certain unshakable magick in doing things by the book, even if one rationally knows that doing so is unnecessary. In my own book *Planetary Spells*

& Rituals, I ask readers not to perform any spell in the book precisely as it is written—though I'd be foolish to think it wouldn't happen! Part of the magick is, after all, in the gathering of components and the exactitude of artfully crafting one's subtle energy. Take the spells given in the *Papyri Graecae Magicae* (Greek

Magical Papyri), for instance. These ancient Greco-Egyptian spells utilize extreme precision—and a whole host of extreme, bizarre, and freakishly unusual ingredients and procedures—in order to produce a desired outcome.

I believe a balance can be struck between the "do it all intuitively" and the "do it all as it's written" spheres. The way I do this is by relying on essential, common base ingredients or components for making magick. If practitioners allow themselves to utilize widely usable components in their magick, it provides a foundation for additional ingredients to be utilized that may be more specialized in nature. For example, I may take advantage of the ever-usable herb mugwort for a spell I wish to create aimed at increasing my psychic abilities. I may place mugwort at the base of a candle, sprinkle it around the house, create a charm bag, or *whatever*. This versatile ingredient will indeed propel my magical intention where I direct it, which in this case is to open my psychic eye, but I may desire a bit more precision and may choose to add some cinquefoil to the mugwort (to psychically shield myself from attack) or may add some deadly nightshade (in order to psychically see through the darkness) or a meticulous combination of ingredients based on ancient spells or simply based on my own intuition. As these examples show, a person can utilize a common base ingredient as the foundation for a working, but may add additional components to the spell in order to gain more precision—more focus—in the magickal act.

> I believe a balance can be struck between the "do it all intuitively" and the "do it all as it's written" spheres. The way I do this is by relying on essential, common base ingredients or components for making magick.

Spell Components

Components listed here draw from numerous cultures. If a Witch or magician is practicing spellcraft with only a handful of ingredients, or desires to craft spells or charms on a budget, may this (partial) list serve as a suggestion for some of the most versatile, widely used, or otherwise effective components in magickal crafting.

ALTAR

The altar is the centerpiece to spellcraft or magickal work performed in a ceremonial setting. Nature magick operates a bit differently, not requiring any sort of humanmade structure, whereas the altar is a centerpiece of ceremonial ritual (from which Wicca and other Neo-pagan expressions derive, in part). The altar can be one similar to the Gardnerian design or can be created in an intuitive fashion. It can be dedicated to certain gods, elements, or forces of nature. It can be a collection of personally significant items that a practitioner likes to meditate beside. The possibilities are endless!

ATHAMÉ

One of the traditional working tools of the Craft, the athamé's use is similar to that of the magickal sword, which has uses in Renaissance magick and other ancient systems. This double-edged blade is used to cast a circle, direct energy, and aid in invocation, and may be used as a substitute for a sword or wand.

BELL

The sound of a bell can be used to cleanse an area of energy or can be used to attune to a particular vibration (each chakra is said to vibrate to a different tone, for example). The shaft portion of a bell may be said to represent the phallic or God principle, while the circular portion can be said to represent the vaginal or Goddess principle. The combination of these forces is the Great Rite, energetically bonding the frequencies of reality into one cohesive sound.

Book of Shadows

Whether in a small notebook, a file on the computer, or a parchment-filled monster of a book, keeping a record of one's magickal workings is essential for documenting experiences. Traditional Wicca requires students to hand-copy their teacher's books, which include rituals, mythologies, and practices within one's training system. Solitary practitioners may choose to create their own books or documents, which can be a magickal hodgepodge of anything the practitioner wishes.

Candles

Candles are one of the most basic tools used in spiritual traditions across the globe. Whether formed of paraffin, beeswax, or another natural substance, the light of the candle represents Yod, a Hebrew letter meaning "flame." This Light of God represents the dawning of consciousness and the fiery energy of transformation. Candles represent all elements: fire (flame), earth (solid wax), air (vapor), and water (dripping wax), and may be inscribed, anointed, dressed, or otherwise imbued with any prayer. It's ideal to ignite a candle while performing minor prayers or spellwork, or to honor the dead.

Dead Bugs

A Witch should always have some dead bugs on hand! Bugs should never be killed for this purpose, but should instead be found naturally. As magickal objects, bug carcasses may be used for any sort of banishing spell: as the insect has cast away its mortal coil, the magician likewise casts someone or something from his or her life.

Gemstones

Extremely popular in New Age healing circles, gemstones vibrate to different frequencies and can be used to aid in the healing or realignment of virtually any issue. Stones have rich histories across cultures, so ancient meanings, folk uses, and superstitions mixed with modern interpretations give rise to an incredible assortment of uses for gemstones. While quartz crystal is perhaps the most commonly used and versatile, the thousands of other stone varieties available on the market can be additionally utilized to help one direct and increase energy toward virtually any intention.

Mugwort

As one of the most versatile Witch's herbs, this relative of the wormwood plant has its most prevalent association in the realm of psychic or divinatory ability. Mugwort can be kept near one's tools of divination to aid in the process, can be drunk as a tea, or can be used in any other crafty way to help open the mind's eye. This herb is aligned to Venus and Neptune and is ruled by the element of earth.

Musical Instruments

More ancient than words, natural music can be played at varying tempos to invoke or cast away certain energies during any act of magick or theurgy.

Oil

Oil is used for anointing one's forehead, candles, tools, or anything else. Good all-purpose oils are olive oil and mineral oil, and those that are derived from plant sources each have a different vibration. When selecting oil, ensure that you get one that's *essential* (all-natural ingredients) rather than *fragrant* (contains toxic chemicals).

Pendants

Keep certain enchanted charms in your pocket or around your neck or wrist to remain constantly connected to the Divine, or to whatever energies you intend, throughout the day.

Rose

The "lotus of the west" is used in all manner of spells involving love and lust, and is a truly indispensable component for the magickal practitioner. Sacred to Aphrodite and other goddesses of love, this fragrant flower can also be used to increase empathy and beauty, as well as to encourage peaceful harmony in any situation. Rose is aligned to the planet Venus and the element of water.

Sachet Bags

It is essential to have on hand a variety of muslin, cotton, flannel, and other all-natural bags for the purpose of creating medicine bags and charm bags for oneself and those who may ask for magickal assistance.

Salt

Salt is a standard and important part of magickal ceremony, and represents the element of earth. Salt can be used to consecrate a ritual space or cleanse an area of negative energies. Added to water, salt's cleansing properties can be taken far—particularly in bath water. Sea salt is typically smiled upon more than rock salt, due to its direct association with the ocean: the womb of the earth.

Storm Water

Storms are intense, chaotic, and forceful. These mystical forces-to-be-reckoned-with can be captured in essence through their rainfall.

The water can be added to any spell requiring an added kick or a potent magickal send-off. One can collect storm water simply by putting pots and pans outside during a thunderstorm.

SUGAR

Sugar is used magickally to "sweeten up" people or situations that have become embittered. Sugar can be used in spells of love and happiness. When purchasing sugar, I recommend either raw sugar or pure cane sugar, as opposed to simply "sugar," which is actually the sugar extracted from beets and is most likely genetically modified (which may contaminate not only the physical body, but also one's magickal work).

VINEGAR

Due to vinegar's sour taste, it can be used to "sour" situations for other people, cursing them into unsatisfactory dispositions. While this use dips into black magick, most practitioners who use vinegar take advantage of its cleansing properties. Seeing as it disinfects on the physical plane, it dually has a deep cleansing effect on one's astral body and can be thusly added to a bath (for oneself) or to a floor wash (for one's house and home).

WAND

The magick wand is used for directing energy and consecrating a ritual circle. Instructions for which woods to use and which lengths to have for wands, as well as rituals for harvesting wands, permeate ancient grimoires and books of metaphysical instruction. Sacred wands, including the legendary caduceus of Hermes, have had prominence in numerous ancient cultures and are not restricted to usage within modern Witchcraft movements.

. . . .

Witches and magicians don't necessarily *need* any of the aforementioned components to weave magick into the universe and make true change happen in the world. We really don't. But it's fun, it's arcane, it's nostalgic, it's conducive, and it's cathartic. These versatile ingredients can be used for a multitude of purposes, so keeping them on hand can aid in any metaphysical situation that may arise. By using our Craft, yet not becoming attached to its parts, we can more easily make our wishes come alive and successfully aid in progressing the planet, one step at a time.

Raven Digitalis (Missoula, MT) *is the author of* Planetary Spells & Rituals, Shadow Magick Compendium, *and* Goth Craft, *all published by Llewellyn. He is a Neopagan Priest and cofounder of the "Eastern Hellenistic" magickal system and training coven Opus Aima Obscuræ (OAO), and is a radio and club DJ of Gothic and industrial music. Raven holds a degree in anthropology from the University of Montana and is also a professional Tarot reader, animal rights activist, and performance artist. He is the co-owner of Twigs & Brews Herbs, specializing in bath salts, herbal blends, essential oils, soaps, candles, and incenses. He has appeared on the cover of* newWitch *magazine and* Spellcraft *magazine. Contact Raven at www.ravendigitalis.com or www.facebook.com/ravendigitalisauthor.*

Illustrator: Kathleen Edwards

Magical Transformations

Positive Magic for
Negative Situations

James Kambos

As practitioners of magic, we are familiar with the Witches' moral code of ethics. It's known as the Wiccan Rede, and I've included it here in this ancient rhyme:

> Eight words the Witches' Creed fulfill:
> If it harms none, do what you will.

In other words, do what you want, but don't hurt anyone—this includes you.

Sounds simple, doesn't it? But is it that simple?

Let's face it, life isn't that simple. When things are going smoothly and we are surrounded with peace, love, and financial security, it's easy to be gracious and forgiving. But when we are faced with things such as job loss, illness, divorce, hurtful gossip, or even death, then it is so tempting to resort to negative magic to solve the situation.

We've all had to deal with a creepy boss, a lazy coworker, a nosy neighbor, a back-stabbing friend, and let's not forget those rotten ex-lovers! But I must remind you—this is easier to say than to put into practice—there really is no place for negative or "black" magic in Wicca or any other Pagan faith.

I guarantee it will come back and bite you on the butt when you least expect it. What goes around really *does* come around.

One of the reasons I wanted to write this article is because I'm disturbed by the growing number of websites devoted to revenge spells. You name it, and they've got a revenge spell for it. I've seen sites that have spells to get back at everything from a cheating spouse to a gossipy neighbor. All you need to do is click and—presto!—you've gotten even with your enemy. These sites are dangerous, and I wouldn't touch them with a ten-foot broomstick! First of all you're dealing with negative magic, and you have no control over it. The last thing you need to have is a negative spell bouncing around cyberspace. You don't know what could happen, and the karmic backlash could be disastrous.

As magical people, we have more ways of dealing with any negative energy directed toward us than most individuals. And with this knowledge

As magical people, we have more ways of dealing with any negative energy directed towards us than most individuals. And with this knowledge comes a great responsibility.

comes a great responsibility. It's all right to use our magical knowledge, spells, and rituals to defend ourselves, but we should use only positive magic to weaken and deflect any negativity directed at us. In this way we can protect ourselves, our homes, and our families by creating a type of invisible protective shield.

I've found that when negative situations arise requiring us to defend ourselves magically, they usually fall loosely into one of the following categories:

- Home/neighbors/gossip

- At the workplace

- With former lovers/spouses

- The occasional run of bad luck when you don't know the source

Let's take a look at each of these situations and how you can handle it with positive magic. Where possible, I've included personal experiences.

Protecting Your Home

We've all had to deal with a grumpy, nosy, or gossipy neighbor. I know I have. I once lived next to a very negative person who never had a good word to say about anyone. What did I do to magically defend myself? To protect myself, I turned my home into an oasis of color and beauty. I began to learn about the magical meanings of flowers, herbs, trees, and shrubs. I used them to my advantage.

Facing my neighbor's yard, I planted a pink lilac. Lilacs were originally used to repel evil. Next I planted a large border of wildflowers to attract butterflies, bees, and birds. Along my fence I planted a large climbing rose to promote peace. Near my deck each year I plant Heavenly Blue morning glories. As they climb over my deck, they protect my home from negative vibrations.

Not only did I block my neighbor's stares, I also blocked her dark energy. The amazing thing is that many of my flowers bloom facing my neighbor's yard, like they understand why I planted them.

To stop neighborhood gossip, try this. Fill an old sock with an odd number of protective herbs—I've used Joe-Pye Weed, monarda, and lavender—then tie it up, bury it, and let it rot. As the contents decompose, the gossip will lessen.

Another ancient standby is the Witch ball, or garden gazing globe. Charge it with a protection spell, wipe with rose water, and place near your property line. Any negativity will be harmlessly deflected.

Protection Magic at Work

Performing protection magic in the workplace can be tricky. You want to keep it low-key, and you normally can't use any of your usual magical tools. But here are a few magical tricks for you to try.

If you have a coworker who constantly gives you grief, just turn their negativity back on them. This is similar to the garden gazing globe spell mentioned earlier. Cleanse a small travel mirror with a solution of wormwood and water. At work, place it in your desk drawer, or some other secluded spot, facing in the direction of your coworker. Whatever they do, or say, will go back to them.

To promote more positive energy at work, magically charge a rose quartz crystal. At work, use your rose quartz as an attractive paper weight—no one will suspect your magical intentions.

To stop office gossip, try this. Fold a blank piece of paper in half; visualize the gossip being trapped in the paper as you fold it. Next staple the three loose edges closed and throw the paper away.

If the situation between you and your boss has become tense, or if the general office atmosphere has become toxic, this calls for a cleansing ritual. To do this, arrive at work before anyone else. Bring with you a small amount of saltwater you've blessed. Sprinkle everywhere—corners, doorways, cubicles, etc. This should help. I did this all around my workplace once, the morning after a coworker was fired. Things soon returned to normal.

Protection Against a Former Lover

This is an area where many people get themselves into trouble. The urge to lash out and get revenge seems strongest when an ex-lover is involved. When people ask me to help them get back at a former lover or spouse, I patiently explain to them that karma will take care of it. In the meantime I tell them, instead of getting even, they should concentrate on getting over their ex. Here are some positive magical practices I've suggested.

Let's begin with this magical quickie. Take a photo of you and your former romantic partner and (if you haven't already) tear it in half. On the half that contains your ex's image, rub it with salt and throw it away!

For a cleansing ritual, try this. Write down in blue ink all the hurt and anger you feel. Pour your heart out—no one is going to see this but you. When you feel you've said everything, soak this paper in a clear bowl or glass of water overnight. The next day, pour the water onto the ground and bury the paper.

To rid yourself of feelings for your ex-partner and to prevent further communication, this spell is worth a try. Take two slices of old bread, and in between the slices place the sketch of a broken heart. Tie the slices together with garden twine. During a waning moon, untie the slices and bury the bread and paper in a compost pile, or throw into a stream. In your mind, see your lover's face growing smaller until it's gone.

But, the best positive magic to use to get even with an ex-lover can be summed up in two words: "Live well!"

Protecting Yourself from an Unknown Source

When you've had a run of bad luck and you have an idea who is working against you but you aren't sure, this can make you feel especially uneasy. At a time like this, you must call upon your faith and affirm with all your heart that you can beat this situation with positive magic.

To start, when faced with this kind of attack, begin each morning by facing east and, with your power hand, trace a pentagram in the air. Say an affirmation for protection, end by turning clockwise, and thank the guardian of each direction for attending your ritual.

I'm a big believer in the cleansing quality of white sage, which you can find at New Age shops or health food stores. Sprinkle it throughout your home. It also attracts positive spirit helpers to you. Burning a ceremonial smudge stick works well, too. Carry it from room to room, and end by passing it over yourself from head to toe, letting the smoke curl about you.

If you feel you're the victim of a curse or psychic attack, here is a simple but powerful candle ritual. On a piece of white paper, write down any of the problems you've encountered. Light a new white candle and as you hold the paper over the flame, say:

Candle light,
And fire light:
As this paper burns,
Let the curse return.

Allow the paper to burn out in a heatproof dish. Sprinkle the ashes away from your home. This weakens any negativity aimed at you.

Above all, at a time like this, get plenty of sleep and exercise and eat well. Also pay attention to messages contained in any dreams.

. . . .

When you utilize positive magic to solve a negative situation, you rise above the person who caused you the hurt and pain. You also have the satisfaction of knowing you've followed the Witches' moral code of ethics. The world would be a better place if people of all faiths practiced these simple but powerful words:

Eight words the Witches' Creed fulfill:
If it harms none, do what you will.

James Kambos is a solitary. A regular contributor to Llewellyn's annuals, he is interested in folk magic traditions of the Near East and Appalachia. He makes his home in Ohio.

Illustrator: Jennifer Hewitson

The Dynamics of Mastery: Making the Jump from Beginner to Seasoned Pro

Tess Whitehurst

For me, making the transition from beginner to more advanced magical practitioner wasn't exactly the easiest thing in the world. Though it's my intention to never stop learning and deepening my relationship with my craft, I'm happy to say that I'm finally past that exceptionally uncomfortable stage that I encountered after the initial novelty of magic started to wear off. If you're having a similar challenge with that confusing gray area between beginner and veteran, it's likely that the following insights will help.

Stage 1: Magical Mind, Beginner's Mind

Similar to the overarching message of Shunryu Suzuki's perennial Buddhist classic, *Zen Mind, Beginner's Mind*, as well as the ubiquitous folk belief in what we call "beginner's luck," being a magical rookie is accompanied by a whole treasure chest full of gleaming benefits. First, at this stage, the jump from the mundane into the magical is quite recent. That means that the magic of magic itself is still fresh in your mind, and the excitement of it all lends exponential strength, potency, and beauty to your rituals and spells. Also, because you are still completely new to the game, you don't have much of a concept yet—and you haven't had any time to formulate theories about—how magic works exactly, or about the underlying dynamics of it all. What this means is that it's a bit easier for your belief in the process to be absolute. All you know is that you do a spell and you're supposed to receive your desire, so you trust that it will be so. Will it arrive in a poof of smoke like it does in the movies? Who knows? Maybe it will!

As a result of this humble trust, which allows us to instantly transcend the conventional view of reality as a fairly dreary and mundane thing, our early magical endeavors are often blessed with a generous, and seemingly miraculous, helping of success—not to mention a great deal of fun.

Stage 2: Who Is That Man Behind the Curtain?

In time, however, we begin to notice some of the energetic nuts and bolts of the magical process. You do the love spell, and your new love interest does *not* arrive in a puff of smoke. But you *do* begin to feel more loving toward yourself. You begin to care for yourself with greater levels of attention and adoration. You exercise more and begin to feel more vibrant. Then, you feel really drawn to take a tango class, and there you meet the person of your dreams. Because you are magnetic, this person is drawn to you. Because you are on the alert for your ritual to succeed, you notice and respond to his or her interest. Puff of smoke it may not be, but magical? Certainly. It's just that magic is quite a bit more natural than it's popularly made out to be. *Supernatural* technically means beyond, above, or outside of nature. But magic, we discover in this stage, is not that. Rather, it is a method of aligning with nature itself—our own nature, and that of the universe, which are one and the same—for the purpose of experiencing that which we'd most like to experience.

So what is so challenging about this stage? Although the true nature that lies at the heart of magic is, and always will be, beyond linear thinking and logical understanding (as in the Joseph Campbell quote "God is a metaphor for that which transcends all levels of rational thought"), when we begin to glimpse the man behind the curtain, and then we see that he is *us*, or that the success of any given magical endeavor is largely based on our own anticipation and belief that it will come to pass, our faith in the process can begin to falter—especially when the freshness of the whole practice of magic has begun to fade a bit. The mojo that felt so palpable at the beginning starts to diminish, and our relationship with the process can begin to feel somewhat frustrating and self-conscious. In other words, we may find ourselves pining for the days when we half-expected the puff of smoke.

The underlying challenge, of course, is that although we have begun to observe the dynamics of the magical process, we are still trapped in the dualistic and language-based, linear thinking that is so prevalent in our species at this period in our evolution. We still feel that it's accurate to mentally delineate between dual aspects, and we truly believe that they are utterly separate from each other: form/spirit, mundane/magical, seen/unseen, cause/effect. As much as we may give lip service to the idea that "everything is connected," we still feel fundamentally separate from the universe, and from everything in it, and even from magic itself. If there's no puff of smoke—we

can't help but feel—there may just be no magic after all. The idea that it's all been tantamount to whimsical wishful thinking stalks us and threatens to undermine our joy. As we pine for "the beginner's mind that was," we may even find ourselves vacillating between depressive emptiness and manic fantasy.

Stage 3: Rising from the Ashes

The good news is that magical practitioners and phoenixes have a lot in common. Those moments of unexplainable transcendence and seemingly miraculous success that we experienced in stage 1 can inspire us to doggedly persist through stage 2 until we get to the other side, much like the fading memory of rising from the ashes might inspire the phoenix to remain on the pyre through yet another blaze.

And what do we experience when we rise from the ashes into stage 3? No more mundane, only magical. Our mind, and the sensory perceptions that we receive through the filter of our mind (we finally realize), simultaneously contain the entire universe and are contained within the entire universe. There

is, *truly*, no separation. We begin to see that the waves of thought, feeling, and vibration that make up our entire life experience are both within us and all around us, and we then become empowered to dance with them and channel them so that they take the physical and emotional forms that we desire. Our magic becomes a joyful, inextricably intertwined co-creation with the universe itself, not just when we are doing a ritual, but also every second of every day: when we are dreaming, washing the dishes, painting, watching a sunset, reading the news, or petting the cat. It's like the subtitle of veteran magician Lon Milo Duquette's autobiographical book, *Low Magick*: "It's All in Your Head … You Just Have No Idea How Big Your Head Is."

It's interesting to note that you may find that you do fewer rituals in stage 3, as the realm of magic and the realm of mundane become inextricably linked in your consciousness. It's almost as if your entire life becomes one big spell, every activity becomes a ritual, and your ongoing stream of consciousness becomes one big incantation.

If you are still in stage 2, of course, this all probably sounds like a nice idea but not like something that you really understand on an experiential level. In another way, it might sound like a disappointing philosophical downgrade from the cinematic, nose-twitching, wand-brandishing skill that you hoped magic could be when you were still in stage 1. Once you arrive in stage 3, however, you will see very clearly that it is neither of these. Rather, stage 3—and magic itself— is an alignment with, and navigation of, the flow of life in a way that feels deeply nourishing and satisfying on every level, and in a way that allows you to continually steer toward, and experience, the blessings and life conditions that you authentically and organically desire.

How to Get There from Here

Of course, every magical practitioner's journey is different. But here are a few things that helped me to transition from stage 2 to stage 3, and then to joyfully and diligently persist in my third stage magical practice. (Because—did I mention?—it's ideal to look at it as an ongoing thing, like practicing an instrument or a sport.)

1. Start with the So-Called Mundane

If I had to name one single thing that helped me the most with making the jump into stage 3, it would be clutter clearing. But not just any clutter clearing: clutter clearing with the awareness that everything is connected, and that our outer environments mirror our inner environments, and vice versa. When I went through such a physical process with the seemingly mundane items in my home while seeing it also as an utterly spiritual/emotional healing process, as well as a process of clearing away the invisible blocks to my most ideal life conditions, my mentally constructed separation between "mundane" and "magical" began to wane. Especially when I felt an immediate, palpable energy and mood boost and when everything in my life began to rapidly flow in a more positive and pleasant direction. My conscious clutter-clearing process took the concept of "everything is connected" and made it into a direct, tangible experience. In other words, it was no longer something I had to believe in, because I saw it in action, and felt it, very clearly.

Along the same lines, when you think of something that you usually consider "mundane," such as washing the dishes, and choose to make it into a magical act, you're helping to eradicate the illusion that anything is ever really mundane (because, of course, it's not). Naturally, there will be times when your mind will drift, and mopping the floor will be a drudgery. But when, again and again, we return our awareness to the Divine, and to the fundamental connection between the seen and the unseen, we practice magic in action and dive into the real truth: everything is connected, everything is magical, and we are utterly empowered to shape our destiny according to our desires.

But how to do this? By simply setting the intention, sweeping the floor can be a ritual to clear away the old to make room for the new: for prosperity, romance, clarity, or any conditions that you'd presently like to experience. Clearing the table after dinner can be an act of devotion when you dedicate your efforts to the goddess of bounty as a way of giving thanks for a delicious meal. Feeding your cats can be a loving offering to both your beloved furry family members and the entire web of life. Taking a shower can be a powerful method of cleansing and activating your aura and chakras.

> ... when you think of something that you usually consider "mundane," such as washing the dishes, and choose to make it into a magical act, you're helping to eradicate the illusion that anything is ever really mundane ...

2. PRACTICE HUMILITY EVEN WHILE KNOWING YOU ARE DIVINE

Once we get into stage 3, there are many things that are utterly true that sound like contradictions. This is because language is not suited to describe the Divine or divine conditions, as language, by its very nature, makes things into one thing and not another thing. Contradictions arise when we are talking about magic/divine energy because the divine does not exclude, and conditions within it cannot be delineated.

One of these contradictions is that you are utterly unique and totally deserving of love and all the very best that life has to offer — even so, you are nothing special. Similarly, even though on one level you are omniscient and omnipotent (in the sense that you are one with the Divine and the flow of magic itself), within the appearance of time and your present physical incarnation (which may both be seen as illusions of a sort), there are many things that you do not know and cannot immediately change. When we become honest about all of this—feeling and sensing our divine nature while also recognizing and honoring our limits and not seeking to behave as if we, individually, are more powerful than we actually are—we can flow more har-

moniously with the part of us that is divine rather than the part of us that is limited and human. For example, if you are in a boat and you insist on paddling against the current in order to prove how powerful you are, you will not experience much pleasure or success. If, on the other hand, you choose to flow *with* the current rather than against it, acknowledging its power and letting your flow become one with its flow, your nautical endeavor will be much more likely to be both victorious and exhilarating. So magic, in stage 3, can often be about recognizing and trusting the invisible flow within the pattern of your life and the universe, so that you can allow it and ride along with it rather than fight against it or try to shape it for the purpose of proving your individual magical prowess, to yourself or anyone else.

It can also help to remember that, even though we magical practitioners are often, admittedly, exceptionally bright by the standards of the world, since everyone is highly intelligent in their own unique way, everyone we meet is almost certainly smarter than we are in at least one important regard (and probably more). Doing our best to listen to and respect everyone we meet will always reap immediate and lasting rewards. Not to mention, when we see every single thing as an expression of the Divine and an extension of ourselves, we begin to also see that every person and every experience is our perfect spiritual teacher, providing exactly what we need in this moment in order to heal, grow, and deepen our alignment with our own divine power. (This is not to say that we should not seek to shift undesirable conditions or speak our truth even if others disagree—it is just to say that looking at each situation as a perfect opportunity and a reflection of the Divine is the most helpful starting point.)

Incidentally, volunteering in a way that allows you to directly be of service to others who are in need of help—such as serving food to people who are homeless or taking a shelter dog for a walk—can be a wonderful way to practice being both divine and humble at the same time. Additionally, consciously directing your effort toward a particular deity, or toward the web of life and/or universal energies in general, will increase the karmic boomerang effect. (In other words, what you send out always comes back to you, especially when you act with intention, devotion, and a respectful awareness of the interconnection of all things.)

3. Have Patience, Be Persistent, and Let Healing Yourself Be a Lifelong Art

Most likely, the transition from stage 2 to stage 3 won't happen overnight. However, now that you're a bit more aware of the dynamics of the process, you can make the transition into a fun magical project. In fact, an important aspect of stage 3 is seeing all challenges as grist for the transmutation mill, and as opportunities to learn, grow, heal, and continually deepen our alignment with divine magical power. So have patience with the process, stick to it, and constantly be on the lookout for new opportunities to heal and grow. Remember, the universe is a mirror of your divine nature, and vice versa. So when you heal, everything benefits. And when you deepen your wisdom and align more solidly with your natural current of magical power, everything evolves. It's all a part of the process.

Tess Whitehurst *is the author of* Magical Housekeeping, The Good Energy Book, The Art of Bliss, *and* The Magic of Flowers. *She writes and teaches about the connection between form and spirit, seen and unseen, known and unknown. Her message is that we are completely empowered to heal ourselves and others, to live bravely, and to create the life of our dreams. To learn more about her work, to view her events, and to sign up for her free monthly newsletter, please visit www.tesswhitehurst.com.*

Illustrator: Rik Olson

Making Magical Water

Dallas Jennifer Cobb

In North America we take water for granted. We have lots to drink and bathe with, and rarely face shortages. We can buy spring, mineral, and even vitamin water in corner stores. But where do we get magical water? Can any water be used, or is some water more magical than others? How is magical water made?

I live beside Lake Ontario and know the magical power this large body of water exudes. Pagan author Starhawk defines magic as "the power to change energy at will," and water changes human energy—emotional, physical, spiritual, and mental. Perhaps this is why water is used in sacred rites and rituals in almost every faith known.

Water can change our energy, and water itself can have its energy changed. It can be "charged" so that its essential energy becomes something more than ordinary water. Water can be assigned a specific purpose, power, or vibration, making it "magical" water to use for clearing, blessing, cleansing, purification, and even healing.

Simple Science

Everything is made of tiny electrically charged particles, both positive and negative, called ions. We assume "positive" means good and "negative" means bad, but with ions, it is reversed. Negative ions are the good ones.

Both positive and negative ions occur naturally, but there are more sources of positive ions, which can create an imbalance in our environment, surroundings, and bodies. Unpaired positive ions are sometimes called free radicals and are highly reactive. Attempting to neutralize their charge, positive ions bond with anything at hand. Imagine the quick fouling of water by pollution, or how electromagnetic energy can cause cell mutation, leading to cancer.

Positive ions are produced by high voltage networks, heating and cooling systems, electrical appliances, engine exhaust, pollution, radiation, and toxins. With so many sources of positive ions all around, it's important to create sources of negative ions in order to balance the pairs of electrons.

Wonderful Water

Each water molecule (H_2O) is made of two hydrogen atoms and one oxygen atom, held together by mild electromagnetic charges. The water molecule is neutral, but because positive and negative charges aren't distributed uniformly in the three-atom structure, the extra hydrogen can "stick" to other elements quite easily. Water molecules stick easily to one another, and to every other "organic" substance they contact, making water the "universal solvent."

Breaking the surface of water—by wave action, waterfalls, misting, or evaporation—disrupts the H_2O molecule, releasing negative ions into the atmosphere. These ions bond with free radicals (positive ions), neutralizing them, with beneficial health effects, such as improved air quality, restored acid/alkaline balance, and neutralized toxins.

Areas where there's a natural occurrence of negative ions are places most people enjoy and seek out: waterfalls, oceans, and rushing rivers. But even if you don't live near a natural source, you can easily create negative ions, facilitating the balancing and healing of yourself and your environment. Running a humidifier, atomizer, mister, mini-waterfall, or water feature creates an abundance of negative ions. And when you're in need of immediate help, just step into the shower or bath.

Pure Water Sources

When working with water, it is best to use pure water. It could come from dew, rainwater, spring water, snow, or the ocean. Use morning dew for blessing, healing, recovery, and beauty spells. Collect it before sunrise on a sabbat for increased energy.

For purification, clearing, protection, and safety, use spring water. To clear grief, shock, fear, or anger, go to the source of the Goddess: the spring.

Because of its high salt content, ocean water is wonderful for bodily energy clearing. Start with a clean slate, and immerse yourself in the ocean. Consecrate new magical tools, jewelry, and garments in ocean water. Or use it for deep spiritual cleansing, to get rid of "evil" spirits.

Rain is associated with abundance, growth, crops, and fertility (of both plants and people). When the skies open up, don't run indoors, but turn your face up, open your arms, and welcome the abundance of the Goddess. Gather water in glass or earthenware (clay) vessels, and strictly avoid plastic, which has its own volatile energy that is easily imprinted on water. Use large glass jars with glass caps, the kind commonly used for home canning. Using a simple rubber strip to create a seal, the vessel is entirely glass, and very neutral energetically. To collect rainwater or dew, use a large earthenware bowl, left outside during a shower or overnight. Gather the water early in the morning.

In the winter, you can gather and melt snow. This water is excellent for promoting peace, calm, and quiet. Use it to make a remedy for sleeplessness: snow water infused with chamomile.

Pure water can also be charged with the energy of elements or planets. Moon water amplifies belief, accentuates intuition and visions, and aids dreamwork. Sun water instills energy, strength, clear purpose, and confidence. Place the open vessel of water out overnight during the phase of the moon you want, or midday during the height of the sun, to engage the planetary energy. Pour water into a sealing glass vessel, then close and label.

Purifying Water

If you live in an urban area without access to the outdoors to collect natural water, you may depend on tap water. Do not fear—it can be used by first purifying it.

There are several ways to purify water. One is to focus your intention on the energetic purification of the water, using the technique outlined in the next section. Alternately, you can let water sit overnight so that evaporation dissipates the amount of chlorine and fluoride, or you can use a carbon filter system (like Brita) to remove the larger particles in the water.

Charging Water

While water can be charged generally with the energy of elements and planets, specific intention is the most powerful ingredient for making magical water. To raise its vibration, hold the open vessel containing the water in your hands. Clear your mind, and with a few deep breaths, focus on the task you want the water to perform.

Feel that particular energy flow through your body, from your head to your heart and out your hands. Envision the energy as a color, or a vibration, or even words. Let these flow through you and into the water. In your mind's eye, see the energy enter the water and bond with hydrogen molecules.

> While water can be charged generally with the energy of elements and planets, specific intention is the most powerful ingredient for making magical water.

Lean close to the water and whisper the task so that your breath touches the water and creates ripples. Whether you imbue water with blessings (love, joy, abundance, and security), clearing (removing negativity, protection, safety, and the creation of positive forces), or healing (antiseptic, antibiotic, disease-free, or recovery), its work is all the same—negative ions are empowered to bond with positive ions and neutralize their damaging effect.

Charged water can be used daily to cleanse tools; protect doorways, gates, property, and home; and bless children, partners, pets, and self. Sprinkle charged water over people, pets, and places. Mop floors and wipe counters with it, and immerse tools in it while intoning the charged energy.

High "Prana" Water

Not just for external application, water can be charged to carry specific energy, and be consumed. *Prana* is another word used to describe energy, so high prana water is high-energy water, charged or imprinted with specific energy. In *Spiritual Nutrition*, author Gabriel Cousens says, "Healing water is high-*prana*, structured, positive energy water." By charging the water, it's possible to alchemically transform it into healing water, raising its vibration and increasing its magical efficacy and power.

Use pure water that doesn't already have a lot of energy attached to it. Pure water retains its neutrality, which makes it easier to charge with specific energy. Lake water may contain mineral particles, and tap water could contain copper pipe particles, fluoride, or chlorine. Use pure spring water (from a spring, not from a bottle), rain water, snow water, or dew. Raise its vibration with intention (see previous section), then transfer it to a sealing bottle and label it according to its charge: *Healing*, *Blessing*, or even *Sweet Dreams*.

Drink high prana water mindfully, as needed, focusing on the magical intent of the water. With each swallow, ingest that energy and feel it work within you. To aid recovery from illness, drink healing or recovery water. If you want to boost your self-esteem, drink love water.

Making Magical Water

Charged water and high prana water have their uses, but for spells, rituals, rites, and ceremonies, make your own specific magical water, traditionally made from pure water, salt, herbs, and/or oils.

Work in sacred space, at your altar, in your kitchen, or out somewhere in nature. Ensure your privacy and safety. The practice of casting a circle enables you to scan your environment. Drawing a simple pentagram for protection enables you to easily invoke the elements and directions.

Place the vessel containing water in the pentagram's center. Add a pinch of salt, saying:

I *purify thee.*

Add small bundles of herbs to the water, saying:

I *energize thee.*

I like chamomile (for peace, sleep, ease, and calm), sage (for protection, banishment, and purification), oregano (for healing, recovery, and cleansing), or St. John's wort (to uplift, banish the blues, and bless). Essential oil can be used instead of, or in addition to, herbs, but use only food-grade, nontoxic essential oils for anything you'll consume.

Next, stir clockwise, saying:

I *enliven thee.*

Know you are releasing the powerful negative ions.

Wrap your hands around the vessel. Lean in close, whispering to the water so that your breath touches it, causing ripples. Say:

I *empower thee with* [healing, protection, cleansing, renewal—or whatever you charge the water to do].

In your mind's eye, see the energy of your focused thought move from your brain, through your heart, down your arms, and out your hands. Envision the energy entering the water, charging it. See the hydrogen molecules bonding with the energy of the sacred salt, the spirited herbs, and your good intention. See the water change.

Dip two fingers (index and middle) of your right hand in the water, draw a pentagram in the air above the vessel, and say:

I *transform thee.*

Remove herbs, then transfer the water to a jar and label clearly with the magical intention and the date.

• • • • • • • • • • • •

Make magical water for any purpose, and over time build up a collection to be used to work magic, to transform energy in the environment, in your home, in people, and in yourself.

Blessed be.

RESOURCE

Cousens, Gabriel. *Spiritual Nutrition.* Berkeley, CA: North Atlantic Books, 2005.

Dallas Jennifer Cobb *practices gratitude magic, giving thanks for her magical life, happy and healthy family, meaningful and flexible work, and joyous life. She believes the Goddess will provide time, energy, wisdom, and money to accomplish all her deepest desires. She lives in paradise, in a waterfront village in rural Ontario, and chants: "Thank you, thank you, thank you." Contact her at jennifer.cobb@live.com.*

Illustrator: Tim Foley

(As Close as You Can Get to) Knowing Hecate

Diana Rajchel

The Goddess Hecate, known today as something of a badass Witches' goddess, was in her early days viewed as a goddess of the household and a great ally to women wanting to keep their homes running smoothly. While there are relatively few direct references to her in the annals of Greek myth, she is still quite well known, and her fame may have increased in modern times thanks to well-placed mentions in the works of Shakespeare.

As a household goddess, Hecate saw to the day-to-day lives of her followers, and as a chthonic goddess, her expressions and worship often became complicated behind a shroud of Mystery tradition. While identified as one of the three great goddesses of the Eleusinian mysteries (the others being Kore and Demeter), it's unclear what specific role Hecate plays in the inner story.

Hecate appears most significantly in one story: the abduction of Persephone. After Hades kidnapped Persephone, Hecate was one of only two witnesses to the incident. In one version, she made the grieving mother Demeter laugh, by lifting her skirts and showing her genitals. She also led Demeter through the night in her search for her daughter, lighting the grain goddess's way with torches in the underworld. After Demeter discovered what happened to Persephone, Hecate stayed on as a handmaiden and companion to the bereaved goddess.

While no specific known myth provides the details, the legend of Hecate suggests that she holds the greatest power possible over

Olympus. As the key holder to the mountain residence of the gods, she alone knows how Zeus will die.

Outside of these two mythical annotations, Hecate does not often appear as a leading character in ancient myths. Yet it's clear she stayed in the hearts and minds of her followers. She appears in a great deal of ancient art and scores many a mention in Greek plays. Her priestesses Medea and Circe both make memorable appearances. Medea, a priestess of Hecate, fell to an enchantment by the goddess Aphrodite. Under that enchantment, she helped the hero Jason capture the Golden Fleece and became both tragic heroine and arch-villain.

Circe, on the other hand, beguiles Hercules with sorcery into a cross-dressing party on her private island after she turns his men into swine. Circe represented the wildness and pleasure of sovereign women, gained with skills ruled by Hecate.

While certainly associated with mayhem, murder, and mystery, Hecate also holds keys to tremendous compassion, loyalty, wisdom, healing, and profound self-confrontation. What modern practitioners know of her nature is that she has a sense of humor, and is not concerned with modern convention, but with the heart of meaning in the human experience. Even in ancient Greece, her priestesses broke with traditional roles of female subservience. The aforementioned Medea, as the daughter of a king, already held considerable power. She only gave up her power when Aphrodite cast a spell. When her husband betrayed her, she took all that

While certainly associated with mayhem, murder, and mystery, Hecate also holds keys to tremendous compassion, loyalty, wisdom, healing, and profound self-confrontation.

power back and then some. Circe chose to never give up her power at all—and felt quite comfortable breaking with social and sexual conventions while retaining it.

Hecate has become omnipresent in the Witchcraft practices of the modern day, and experience with her holds something much more complex than that assigned a myth's supporting cast member. Because of her association with Witchcraft and with the moon, she appeals to Wiccans, and her "do what's necessary" attitude appeals to those who practice culture-specific forms of Witchcraft.

As a goddess associated with crossroads, her traditions also blend into a sort of "Americana Witchcraft," as she easily shares associations with traditions that came from oppressed people settled and already present on the American continents. She was a goddess to women in ancient Greece when the law defined all women as property, and something in her speaks to people elsewhere in the world who are defined by others as property.

Despite her modern popularity, Hecate can still be a difficult goddess to know. When she appears in Drawing Down the Moon ceremonies, she does not mince words—and she only rarely gives directions. Hecate requires a great deal of education, and she brooks neither insolence nor dilettantism.

Normally when a person wishes to pursue connection or communion with a god, they are advised to read as much mythology on that god as possible. Although the myth material on Hecate is sparse, it's advisable to seek out anything you can. If you're willing to put the effort into knowing more about her, you're also willing to put the effort into learning the lessons she teaches. What matters most is that you look.

Once you have made yourself as familiar as possible with her myths and symbols, you must spend time understanding not just what Hecate rules over, but also her personality. This is where learning about her becomes tricky, and where you must dive deep into

ancient mythology, looking into hymns and plays, looking at the actions of her priestesses, modern and ancient, and even watching the behavior of animals dedicated to her.

For example, two animals are associated with Hecate: black bitches, and a cousin to ferrets, weasels, and minks known as the polecat (different from the North American colloquialism for "skunk"). In both cases, myth tells that the creatures began as Witches/priestesses to Hecate, and that she transformed them into her familiars for infractions. In the case of the dog, a Witch leapt into the sea at the fall of Troy, so Hecate transformed her. In the case of the polecat, Hecate resolved her human incontinence.

The second phase in engaging with Hecate after learning her myths is to open conversations with her. Most practitioners do this through meditation. When you meditate on Hecate, surround yourself with symbols associated with her. This can include keys, black dogs, marigolds, carnations, and images of doors.

If possible, address your first prayer to her standing under a doorway. To the ancient Greeks, doorways marked the third angle of a crossroads—the road being what went in either direction in front of your house. Ask yourself what sort of person teaches by transforming. Observe what happens at roadways and doors.

When you have moved from introduction to ritual—and expect that to come up fast, as Hecate waits for very little—you should understand that Hecate is not a something-for-nothing-style goddess. While she does not demand sacrifices, if you make a vow to her you better keep it, or she will see to it that you experience consequences. Be a good host when you invite her to ritual, and offer her some incense and a few decent libations.

An ancient method of establishing connection to Hecate required establishing a household shrine. This shrine propitiated a relationship that kept off the forces of ill-intended magic and encouraged prosperity. You can create one yourself, either drawing from reconstructed Hellenic custom or building something more typical of twenty-first-century Wiccans. While a flat surface is preferable, a shoebox mounted on a wall can work as long as you don't use it for anything heavy or that you might wish to burn. Make sure you include an image of Hecate. In the shrine, leave small offerings of flowers, speak a daily prayer before it, and make sure you spend a small amount of time listening to what Hecate might have to say to you. Her words can rattle, and you may disagree, but you will also learn how to have that two-way conversation with the Divine that will influence the rest of your practice.

Learning about Hecate and her infinite associations can take years. Hecate connects with women and men who are fierce, independent, and capable of breaking away from social convention. These are people who bear metaphorical torches lighting the way through new paths.

> **Hecate connects with women and men who are fierce, independent, and capable of breaking away from social convention.**

Hecate requires respect and no small amount of commitment. She is also very sharp and very strong. Be consistent in your communication with her. Show up daily. Keep your word. While we associate her with hours-long rituals and Drawing Down ceremonies, it's the small, daily connections that define a deity/practitioner relationship. Put in the time to know Hecate, to learn her ways and her limits and to accept her challenges. She will know you in turn.

FOR FURTHER STUDY

Theoi Greek Mythology, "Hekate Cult," www.theoi.com/Cult/HekateCult.html.

Internet Sacred Text Archive, "Hymn to Demeter," www.sacred-texts.com/cla/demeter.htm.

von Rudloff, Robert. *Hekate in Ancient Greek Religion*. Victoria, BC: Horned Owl Press, 1999.

Conway, D. J. *Maiden, Mother, Crone: The Myth and Reality of the Triple Goddess.* St. Paul, MN: Llewellyn Publications, 1994.

Diana Rajchel *serves as the executive editor for PNC-News and is the author of* Divorcing a Real Witch: For Pagans and Those Who Used to Love Them. *She is a third-degree Wiccan Priestess in the Shadowmoon tradition, with 17 years of practical experience as a Witch. You can find out more about her by visiting http://blog.dianarajchel.com. Remember that j.*

Illustrator: Bri Hermanson

Bringing the Ancestors into Your Practice

Michael Furie

We hear a lot about the ancestors (both the vast number of our ethnic or spiritual ancestors and our own individual family ancestors) in the Pagan community. Most of us take time out to honor them at Samhain, and some of us honor or connect to them more frequently using various methods. A great many of the methods used to tune in to the energy of our departed loved ones use items and ingredients that some people find spooky or unsettling. Unfortunately, not a lot of information about how to contact, honor, or commune with them in a simple

manner is readily available. In my practice, I have used everyday items as tools to honor the ancestors and will share my ideas and include a ritual sample.

Communing with ancestors and spirits has been associated with Witches for centuries and, indeed, can be one of our many skills. The ancestors can be acknowledged, honored, or called during any of the sabbats or esbats for protective reasons, to communicate with them, or just as a sign of respect and reverence. If you are conducting formal ritual within a magic circle, you can place offerings and tools, such as mirrors or a crystal ball, in the western quadrant of the circle to draw in their energies. This is the natural area of connection to their realm. If you wish, the main altar itself can be situated so that it faces west when working with the ancestors. This alignment will help with the energy flow and connection to their realm. However you decide to arrange your altar and circle, the next question becomes, "What should I place on the altar?"

> **The ancestors can be acknowledged, honored, or called during any of the sabbats or esbats for protective reasons, to communicate with them, or just as a sign of respect and reverence.**

I was taught that spirits see live or freshly cut flowers as glowing "lights," and placing fresh flowers on an altar designed to honor or communicate with them can help call their attention, the flowers acting as a beacon. Fresh flowers could also be placed in the western quadrant of the circle to help call in the ancestors. When placing flowers on the altar, set them at the back of the altar either in the middle or to the left side, being sure to keep them far enough away from any candles that are present. The types of flowers used are not especially important. If desired and available, you could use specific flowers known to help spirit communication, such as jasmine or lavender flowers, or you could use flowers that are known to have been favorites of a particular ancestor if you are trying to attract their attention. If your great-grandmother, for example, was fond of gardenias, using them on an ancestor altar would be a good means of contacting her.

If you are trying to contact specific ancestors, it also helps to have photos and other mementos on the altar (if it is large enough) or, most often, placed in the western quadrant of the circle. The more personal items you have, the better the connection will be, generally speaking. When you actually make your verbal petition to the ancestors during your ritual, it is a good idea to offer them a libation, both out of respect and to lend them life energy to help them cross the bridge into our realm. Honey is excellent to use, as are apple cider, wine, and milk. Food can also be used in conjunction with the liquids. Beans and grains are traditional, cooked or uncooked, as you prefer. Any or all of these offerings are usually poured either into the cauldron or into a special offering bowl and, after the ritual, are poured into a hole dug in the earth.

It must be stated that, unlike the traditional Cakes and Wine ceremony, wherein we share a toast with the gods, it is not a good idea to partake of the food or drink offered to the departed. Use a separate cup and a separate offering bowl or cauldron for the sole purpose of connecting to the energy of the ancestors. If you wish to toast the ancestors, use your usual ritual cup and a separate beverage you have prepared for yourself. The reason for this is that we are using food to lend them the energy of life, and though we may wish to commune with them, we do not want to partake of the energy of death before our time. Why hasten the aging process? Not sharing their food and drink keeps us safe.

Speaking of keeping ourselves safe, it is a good practice to wear a protective amulet when calling on any spirit just in case the wrong one should show up, but it is a bad idea to use salt, even in the circle casting for this ritual. Use the consecrated water, but omit the salt. Salt is repellent to spirits and should only be used in your usual magical or religious workings or when trying to be rid of an unwelcome entity. I don't mean to sound alarmist. In my experience, there is relatively little danger when trying to contact your own ancestors. All you need are some basic precautionary measures, experience in casting circles and running ritual, and a true desire to connect with your ancestors.

The danger in dealing with spirits mainly comes from calling upon any spirit, such as when people "play" with spirit boards, thinking them a joke. When a Witch (or anyone else) sends out a call without specific criteria, it can be answered by whatever willing spirit chooses to manifest. This can be incredibly risky and is not advised. When you send out a call for your ancestors, be specific that you seek only positive, loving communication that will be friendly and mutually beneficial. This statement of purpose lends clear intent to your call and helps to eliminate any unwelcome entities from coming forward.

Okay, so we've established some dos and don'ts and general guidelines, but once you have contacted the ancestors, what do you do with them? Well, if you wish to communicate with them, it is a good idea to use divinatory tools, such as a black mirror or a pendulum. While in circle, hold the pendulum and ask that the ancestors answer your questions, or gaze into the mirror and ask that they send you visions to communicate with you. If you use the mirror, it is a good idea to situate the censer so that some of the incense smoke drifts in front of the mirror; this helps you slip into the proper frame of mind to receive the messages. If you are using a pendulum, just make sure to ask yes-or-no questions. Incidentally, mugwort is a wonderful herb to burn in the censer to boost communication.

Aside from communication and divination, you can also ask your ancestors for their help in guarding your circle, your home, and your family. There are two main ways to do this. The first is to simply ask them to watch over and act as spiritual guardians, and the second is to ask them to help infuse a charm or spell that you cast with their additional power. This is another instance in which using a personal item from a specific ancestor would prove invaluable. If you have an

heirloom piece of jewelry or a watch, for example, that was owned and loved by a specific and departed family member, it can be charged with protective energy while also asking the ancestor to charge it with their spirit energy, and then it could be worn as an amulet. An amulet such as this is not only protective, but also helps to keep the spiritual link between you and your departed loved one strong, which aids communication.

If your main focus is in honoring and acknowledging your ancestors, there are several less formal options from which to choose. Daily or weekly devotions are a lovely means of keeping in touch with them and do not require full-scale ritual or circle casting. You can set up an informal ancestor altar on a bedroom dresser top, if you wish. Personal items, flowers, and photos should be arranged on the altar space in a pleasing manner. Place a white votive or tea light candle in front of each photo, if safe to do so. You can light each candle and say a quick prayer of devotion. It is better to do this in the evening rather than in the morning. The reason for this is that nighttime allows for easier communication; the daytime is usually far too busy.

Setting up a regular routine of devotion creates a rhythmic current and greatly helps to connect to your ancestors on more formal ritual occasions. Whether in formal ritual or nighttime devotion, it is very important to keep in mind that when you are doing this work, you are attempting to contact fully conscious, independent beings, so it is wise to address them as though you were talking to any other person who is alive and well and standing in front of you. We must not be overly demanding or flippant with them, or else we risk offending them and cutting off our own ability to commune with their energy.

Sample Ritual

This snippet of ritual can be included as a part of virtually any ceremony and is given to provide a working example of the steps involved. In this rite, it is assumed that the ancestor photos, personal items, and an offering bowl are placed in the western quadrant of the circle, and that the goal of calling upon the ancestors is to commune with and honor them.

After the circle has been cast and the quarters have been called, return to the west, carrying a cup of libation and/or a dish of food to be offered to the ancestors. When you stand before the western quadrant, declare your intent and affirm your petition with words such as these:

> *Beloved ancestor(s), my/our family line, draw close to me/us on this night.*
> *I call only those who come in peace to commune with me/us and share your light.*
> *Our loving bond, benefiting me/us as well as you,*
> *The veil is lifted, I draw you through.*

Now, pour the libation into the offering bowl (or cauldron) and pour the food (if any) into the offering bowl as well. Take a moment to reach out with your consciousness and *feel* out into the west, and visualize your ancestors coming together as a group (or any specific ancestors drawing near) and responding to your invitation.

When you feel their presence, you can continue with your ritual as planned. It is good form, even during a solitary ritual, when working with your ancestors to say "we" instead of "I" during the rest of your ritual, with the understanding that your ancestors are joining with you in celebration. If you wish to ask your ancestors for assistance, do so after you send out the call in the west, when you feel their presence.

. . . .

All of the techniques presented here can be used at any time of year, though the season of autumn, the sabbat of Samhain, the waning moon, and your own birthdate and/or the birthdates of specific ancestors are special times that can be utilized to boost the current of energy and ease the process of bringing the ancestors through. I hope that I have shown that contacting and working with ancestors is not as spooky or complicated as it sounds. It really is a wonderful endeavor; one that, with continued practice, will bring you many rewards and will greatly enrich your spiritual connections and magical practice.

Michael Furie's *full bio appears on page 36.*

Illustrator: Christa Marquez

Healing Lessons from the School of Life

Laurel Reufner

Sometimes our most deeply felt and profound lessons in life are also the hardest to learn. However, once learned, they stick with us forever. And if we're lucky, we can pass on that hard-won wisdom to someone else, sparing them those particular knocks from life.

I'd like to share with you a couple of life's healing lessons that I had to learn under duress—lessons that reverberated with me in the intervening years that followed. To this day, those lessons affect how I send healing energy to others.

Back in the late 1990s, my stepfather battled a particularly nasty type of prostate cancer. Most forms of prostate cancer are so slow-growing that victims are more likely to die of other causes related to old age than they are from the cancer itself. Not this one. However, it did appear that he'd battled it to a standstill, thanks to a combo of medical science and a wicked sense of humor. Unfortunately, this form of cancer also usually travels hand in hand with a form of bone cancer, with which he was also shortly diagnosed.

I'd been sending vague healing energy his way for quite some time. You probably know what I'm talking about—the kind of energy you send when you remember to do so, or when you happen to be thinking about the person involved. It was sometime after the diagnosis for bone cancer that I got serious. At the time, I had a handmade green candle that contained inclusions of rosemary. Onto my altar went the candle, and I began lighting it daily. I'd spend a few minutes visualizing healing energy winging its way to my stepfather, two hours away from where I lived, and visualize him whole, healthy, and vital once more. Then I'd go off and do whatever while the candle burned for half an hour or so.

Several months after I started this little ritual for my stepfather, I discovered that my high school sweetheart—whom I hadn't seen or spoken to in a long time—was fighting a benign brain tumor. I won't bore you with the details, but suffice it to say that I added him to my healing list. Now I had some serious energy heading in two different directions during my daily healing ritual.

After a while, my health started to suffer. I'd get sick at the drop of a pin. Now, in all honesty, my immune system hadn't been in the best of shape for a long time, partly because I'd spent too much time on antibiotics. However, it hadn't been this bad in a long time. I had a young child in the house and couldn't spend all that time in bed getting over a touch of whatever was going around.

Then it hit me, life's healing lesson number 1. I'd been sacrificing my own health while trying to help my stepfather and former flame. There was nothing wrong with lighting a candle and sending energy fleeting off to someone who was in need, but the spell worker needs to remember to cut that flow of energy at some point during the ritual. Let the energy that's been set loose go off and do its job while you trust in the universe that things are working as they should. In my ritual, the point where I ought to have visualized that energy flow interrupted should probably have been when the candle was extinguished. That one little change made a big difference in how I felt.

Had my healing ritual taken only a few days, there probably wouldn't have been any problems with my own energy being depleted, but since the ritual had been going on for weeks, it became unavoidable. This is something to keep in mind when working your

own healings on loved ones. Remember, you can't be of help to anyone if you're too tired or ill to focus.

At this point, you've probably realized that my story isn't over. After all, I've mentioned a second healing life lesson. Sadly, this lesson had to do with learning to let go and realize that sometimes the time for healing energy has passed.

I'm lucky in that I still had both of my grandmothers and all three of my parents well into my thirties. And when my maternal grandmother died, just shy of the age of ninety, it was because her body just finally gave out. It was all rather quick. My stepfather was a different matter. He fought these cancers for years, in spite of the odds, and he was winning. And he was as close and as important to me as both of my birth parents. So maybe the next of life's healing lessons hadn't occurred to me earlier simply because I'd not yet faced losing anyone quite that important to me.

Remember that prostate cancer we thought my stepfather had beaten to a pulp? Well, apparently if even a single cell is missed, it comes back. And when it does, it comes back with a vengeance. Before we knew it, the rogue cells had entangled his kidneys and were choking them off.

Out came the healing candle again. I started sending healing energy to him once again each day, remembering the first healing life lesson. Then, one day a few weeks before the end, I had a revelation. What if healing energy wasn't what he really needed? What if I might, somehow, only be helping prolong his pain and postponing the inevitable? What if it was time to let go?

I didn't light the candle right away and instead thought about it a bit more. As human beings, we tend to want to help. Christians pray for those who are ill or seriously injured, and we Pagans send energy. Sometimes it may not be much, but I feel sure that it all adds up. Get enough in the positive column and it can perhaps tip the balance to a more favorable outcome.

Sometimes, however, we reach a point where it doesn't matter how many prayers or how much energy gets sent. A point of no return has already been passed and the outcome is inevitable. This was probably one of those times. In spite of everything doctors tried, and in spite of all the healing, protective energy and prayers that would be directed his way, my stepfather's time had come. What does one do in such circumstances? It seems silly to continue praying or sending healing energy to someone whose body can no longer be affected by it.

I eventually lit the candle and sent energy, but it was different this time. This time I offered the healing energy to his soul if it needed it—if it could *use* it. And if the time for such healing was past, then I instead asked his soul to use it to help ease his passing and to make his remaining time with us as pain-free and gentle as possible. I asked that he not suffer. And then I wrapped him in the whitest protective light I could muster up and send. Finally, I cried some for the man who'd been such an influence on my life and whom I had come to love and respect so very much.

My stepfather was a former Marine and a very brave and compassionate man. He was also pretty smart. He probably figured out long before the rest of us that he wasn't going to get better this time. The cancer was winning, and his health had reached a point where any treatments or surgeries were merely serving as stopgap measures that would only prolong his life for small periods of time. Whatever was done couldn't really improve his quality of life. Even dialysis left him feeling weaker and more drained after each session. He finally decided it was time to stop fighting. He made the decision to die peacefully and at home. My mother's only requirement was that he not suffer, that there be no pain. It took him nearly two weeks to make that final journey to the great unknown. Just after hearing his young granddaughters' musical voices one last time, a big wind—heralding a coming blizzard—passed through where he and my mother lived, taking him with it.

And so, dear readers, that is the second healing life lesson I have to share with you. Sometimes, for whatever reason, you can't help a person heal, but just maybe you can help them move on to the next stage in their soul's great adventure. It does require a certain bravery on your part—an ability to let go when you selfishly want to keep them with you. Denying that understandable selfishness can be the hardest thing to do, but sometimes it's also the most compassionate, for both of you.

Blessed be.

> **Sometimes, for whatever reason, you can't help a person heal, but just maybe you can help them move on to the next stage in their soul's great adventure.**

Laurel Reufner's mother can verify that she grew up a "wild child" in farming country. Laurel has been earth-centered for nearly 25 years now and really enjoys writing about shiny topics that grab her attention. She has always lived in southeastern Ohio and currently calls Athens County home, where she lives with her wonderful husband and two wild children of her own. Find her online at oaknolive.blogspot.com.

Illustrator: Kathleen Edwards

Working with Healing Deities

Blake Octavian Blair

In ancient cultures across the globe, magickal folk have often filled the role of the healer in their villages, tribes, communities, and societies. There was the wise woman in her cottage near the woods, the Amazonian shaman deep in the jungle, and the Native American medicine man. European cultures had their own cunning folk. All were sought out for their advice and skill in alternative and spiritual healing through energy, metaphysics, and local plants.

With the growing desire for utilization of natural, complementary, and alternative healing methods, it only makes sense that more people are being called to serve their communities in these areas. Community members also feel more at ease seeking such services and treatments from those within their community who understand, respect, and possibly even share some common ground with their spiritual belief system. Here enters the realm of deity and spirit into the healing equation! In the remainder of this article, we will take a brief look at how to begin exploring healing modalities, and then we'll delve into a few of the healing spirits and deities you could work with and how to go about doing so.

The role of the healer is being filled once again by a new generation of magickal folk who hear the calling to do this important work and to fill this role for their modern communities. Despite the advancement of technology and the passing of time, their fundamental work varies little from that of their predecessors. In fact, modern Pagans who practice the healing arts have the advantage and ability to call upon various methods used around the globe, thanks to the modern technology and travel that has allowed these methods to leave their homelands and reach those who need them. South American shamans are able to travel to Europe and North America to offer insight into their healing practices (and we are able to travel to them as well). Reiki has traveled from Japan across the globe, giving greater access to this incredible healing system and energy. Modern publishing has allowed Native American elders to share their wisdom and philosophy, once contained only in oral traditions, that might otherwise be lost forever. Hoodoo and Rootworkers are able to share their cultural methods through online communities that would otherwise not be possible.

There are a wide range of modalities and training available to the modern magickal practitioner who feels called to the healing arts. Do some research and see what calls to you. Do not take your course of study lightly. Once you find a modality that you feel a connection with and that you wish to pursue, seek resources and appropriate training to become a qualified and knowledgeable practitioner of it. Some modalities and skills are intuitive, such as guided meditation, crystal healing, and healing through prayer and spellwork such as candles. Although formal training and classes are available in these topics and skills, and you may benefit by seeking them out, they are not an absolute requirement for their practice.

Other modalities, such as certain shamanic systems and techniques, Reiki, and Healing Touch, require formal training and/or attunements. In the case of Reiki, for example, the training includes not only the history of the system, practical techniques, and the ethics of practice, but also the required attunements. An attunement is like an initiation of sorts that also serves as an energetic transmission which tunes and aligns the student to the specific energetic vibration. Credible training in shamanic arts and systems not only equips students with the requisite training in practical techniques, but also ensures that the student has learned truthful and correct information and is then able to accurately and confidently utilize the techniques with respect to the cultures from which they came. In any of the healing arts, a wonderful way to learn is to seek out an apprenticeship with a mentor. This will also require a fair amount of research and interviewing to find the mentor that both has the appropriate qualifications and resonates with you.

While corporeal human mentors and teachers on the mortal plane are not to be forsaken, you will also want to explore healing deities and helpful spirits to aid and inspire you in your work and along your journey. There are several ways to go about choosing a deity to partner with in your healing work. You are also not limited to working with only one. An obvious place to start out on your search is to find a deity that is associated with a specific ailment you wish to work on healing. For example, Ogun, a spirit from

the African diasporic traditions, in addition to being a healing spirit, is also seen as a spirit of war and battle. So if, for example, you are looking to treat an ailment that is the result of a military service injury, Ogun would be an excellent choice to pair with.

Although one may not think of nightmares as a condition you "heal," I have had great success in working with Archangel Michael in healing from them. Michael is considered a great protector, and although when it comes to archangels much press for healing is given to Raphael, I know plenty of healing practitioners who work to great success with Michael. As anyone who has worked directly with him can tell you, he is one archangel never to be underestimated!

Yemaya, the mother goddess of Yoruban tradition, can be called upon for the healing of numerous ailments. She is a go-to goddess for anything dealing with the female reproductive system and cycles. If a woman happens to be experiencing any issue related to her monthly cycle, Yemaya has a listening ear and a helping hand to lend. Yemaya's associations with the sea and the cleansing and purifying element of water make her a wonderful link to divine healing energies. An added bonus is that she is seen as a patroness to practitioners of magick and the occult!

The Indic god Ganesha is one of the most versatile deities in the Hindu pantheon. He could be called upon in a variety of capacities for numerous ailments. One of his titles is Remover of Obstacles. This would make Ganesha an ideal deity to help you offer assistance to somebody who is experiencing a blockage such as a blood clot. On a metaphysical level, perhaps the person has a chakra experiencing an energy blockage—Ganesha at your service! Ganesha is a jovial and benevolent god known for assisting all those who approach him with a sincere heart and intent.

Another interesting way to go about choosing a deity to work with is to consider which deity may correspond to or complement your modality. Look to the culture from which the modality you practice originates. My husband and I regularly receive acupuncture treatments. Fascinatingly, acupuncture has an ancient legacy in the East dating back to elaboration of the treatment in a second-century BCE medical text! Our acupuncturist's office is adorned with numerous images of the Medicine Buddha as well as the goddess Quan Yin. Both figure into the Chinese and Japanese cultures of origin for acupuncture, thus making them a perfect fit for practitioners of the field. Practitioners of Reiki, which originated in Japan, are also fond of Asian deities, especially Quan Yin, for similar reasons. She is actually a Buddhist bodhisattva of compassion and mercy, two qualities that should be possessed by those in all healing professions. I myself have a statue of Quan Yin that resides in the room in which I perform healing work.

One of the deities commonly petitioned by Witches for healing is the multifaceted and powerful goddess Hekate. Healer is among her many roles, and she is often asked for assistance in healing when it seems there is no other recourse. There are accounts of miraculous improvements when it seemed all hope was lost and all treatment had been previously unsuccessful. Another goddess of many faces called upon for her healing associations is the Celtic goddess Brigid. Often associated as a goddess of the flame, she is a perfect match for those engaged in the practice of healing through candle burning. In addition, she is also associated with snakes, which have a long-standing association with healing in many different cultures. Both fire and snakes can be seen as symbols of transformation, and through transformation great healing can take place.

A variation of the culture angle is to work with deities that come from either your cultural heritage or that of your client's. For example, if you or your client has Irish ancestry, perhaps Brigid would make a great choice in this instance as well. People of certain Asian heritages might consider working with one of the forms of the goddess Tara. Both White and Green Tara have healing associations.

Perhaps you already have a patron deity that guides and supports you in life. Consider partnering with them for your healing endeavors. You may ask yourself what known connection, if any, the deity has to healing work. Even if you're not readily able to draw a correlation between your patron and healing, don't fret. If you stop, step back, and think about it, your patron already supports you throughout your life activities, so why wouldn't they support your efforts to help not only yourself but also others? Your patron may even surprise you by leading you to another deity that is perfectly suited to assist you in your new efforts! If you feel you need to work with an additional deity more directly suited to your goals, you may wish to look within your patron deity's pantheon at others that may have associations with healing.

You can strengthen your relationship with your healing deities by communicating with them regularly and honoring them with an altar to them and images of them in your healing space. Lighting a candle in front of their image while conducting healing sessions is a simple and effective way to both invoke and honor them. You may also choose to wear a piece of jewelry that corresponds with your deity when doing healing work. Perhaps a cowrie shell bracelet for Yemaya, a Celtic or Brigid's cross pendant for Brigid, or an Om for Ganesha or Tara.

Throughout this discussion I have used language that suggests that the relationship between the healing facilitator and the deity you work with should take on the form of a team effort and partnership. You have to do your own part in facilitating the healing process, and then the deities will be more than happy to do their part in assisting you with their support. It is important to remember that one of the key factors to successful spiritual and magickal work is real-world action. Become a skilled practitioner in your healing art and modality of choice. Be the best you can be, and actually utilize those skills and modalities. Use them to assist yourself and others on a regular basis, whether it be through Reiki, crystal healing, shamanic work, or another method. The gods will most certainly be pleased with your assertiveness, and then, when you petition them to add

You have to do your own part in facilitating the healing process, and then the deities will be more than happy to do their part in assisting you with their support.

their assistance to your existing efforts, the team effort will be a combination that can't be beat. Many of these modalities already incorporate work with the spirit realm within them. If you practice one of those, you are already on your way to developing this partnership.

This is also the perfect time for a reminder that alternative and complementary healing techniques are just that—complementary. They are not a replacement for traditional professional medical and psychological care. Do not discontinue your regular traditional medical treatment with your physicians. Inform your physician of any complementary alternative treatments you may be seeking or administering to yourself. While many traditional physicians and health care professionals are not open to alternative methods, it is important for them to have complete information on what types of treatment you are receiving so they can do their best in assisting you with their own specialties. Be sure to inform those you perform healing work on that it is not a replacement for seeking medical treatment, and instruct them to communicate information regarding their complementary treatments to their physician.

Additionally, before performing healing sessions on others, and especially before setting up a practice, be sure you are legally certified, licensed, and compliant with local laws to offer those services in your area. Different modalities require different types and levels of licensure and registration that can vary from area to area.

Healing work is a much needed, sought after, and gratifying area of service. Consider these famous words spoken by Mahatma Gandhi: "Be the change you wish to see in the world." Wisdom from our predecessors and cultures spanning the globe are within reach. If you are one of those hearing the call to be a modern-day healer, now more than ever you have the resources at hand to answer that call.

FURTHER READING

Alvarado, Denise. *The Voodoo Hoodoo Spellbook*. Scotts Valley, CA: CreateSpace, 2009.

d'Este, Sorita. *Hekate: Her Sacred Fires*. London: Avalonia, 2010.

Glassman, Sallie Ann. *Vodou Visions: An Encounter with Divine Mystery*. 2nd ed. New Orleans, LA: Island of Salvation Botanica, 2000.

Illes, Judika. *Encyclopedia of Spirits: The Ultimate Guide to the Magic of Fairies, Genies, Demons, Ghosts, Gods & Goddesses*. New York: Harper One, 2009.

Blake Octavian Blair's *full bio appears on page 136.*

Illustrator: Jennifer Hewitson

The Lunar Calendar

September 2013 to December 2014

SEPTEMBER
S	M	T	W	T	F	S
	1	2	3	4	5	6	7
8	9	10	11	12	13	14
15	16	17	18	19	20	21
22	23	24	25	26	27	28
29	30

OCTOBER
S	M	T	W	T	F	S
		1	2	3	4	5
6	7	8	9	10	11	12
13	14	15	16	17	18	19
20	21	22	23	24	25	26
27	28	29	30	31

NOVEMBER
S	M	T	W	T	F	S
					1	2
3	4	5	6	7	8	9
10	11	12	13	14	15	16
17	18	19	20	21	22	23
24	25	26	27	28	29	30

DECEMBER
S	M	T	W	T	F	S
1	2	3	4	5	6	7
8	9	10	11	12	13	14
15	16	17	18	19	20	21
22	23	24	25	26	27	28
29	30	31

2014

JANUARY
S	M	T	W	T	F	S
			1	2	3	4
5	6	7	8	9	10	11
12	13	14	15	16	17	18
19	20	21	22	23	24	25
26	27	28	29	30	31

FEBRUARY
S	M	T	W	T	F	S
						1
2	3	4	5	6	7	8
9	10	11	12	13	14	15
16	17	18	19	20	21	22
23	24	25	26	27	28

MARCH
S	M	T	W	T	F	S
						1
2	3	4	5	6	7	8
9	10	11	12	13	14	15
16	17	18	19	20	21	22
23	24	25	26	27	28	29
30	31

APRIL
S	M	T	W	T	F	S
		1	2	3	4	5
6	7	8	9	10	11	12
13	14	15	16	17	18	19
20	21	22	23	24	25	26
27	28	29	30

MAY
S	M	T	W	T	F	S
				1	2	3
4	5	6	7	8	9	10
11	12	13	14	15	16	17
18	19	20	21	22	23	24
25	26	27	28	29	30	31

JUNE
S	M	T	W	T	F	S
1	2	3	4	5	6	7
8	9	10	11	12	13	14
15	16	17	18	19	20	21
22	23	24	25	26	27	28
29	30

JULY
S	M	T	W	T	F	S
		1	2	3	4	5
6	7	8	9	10	11	12
13	14	15	16	17	18	19
20	21	22	23	24	25	26
27	28	29	30	31

AUGUST
S	M	T	W	T	F	S
					1	2
3	4	5	6	7	8	9
10	11	12	13	14	15	16
17	18	19	20	21	22	23
24	25	26	27	28	29	30
31

SEPTEMBER
S	M	T	W	T	F	S
	1	2	3	4	5	6
7	8	9	10	11	12	13
14	15	16	17	18	19	20
21	22	23	24	25	26	27
28	29	30

OCTOBER
S	M	T	W	T	F	S
			1	2	3	4
5	6	7	8	9	10	11
12	13	14	15	16	17	18
19	20	21	22	23	24	25
26	27	28	29	30	31

NOVEMBER
S	M	T	W	T	F	S
						1
2	3	4	5	6	7	8
9	10	11	12	13	14	15
16	17	18	19	20	21	22
23	24	25	26	27	28	29
30

DECEMBER
S	M	T	W	T	F	S
	1	2	3	4	5	6
7	8	9	10	11	12	13
14	15	16	17	18	19	20
21	22	23	24	25	26	27
28	29	30	31

2013
SEPTEMBER

SU	M	TU	W	TH	F	SA
1	2 *Labor Day*	3	4	5 ● New Moon 7:36 am	6	7
8	9	10	11	12	13	14
15	16	17	18	19 ☺ Harvest Moon 7:13 am	20	21
22 *Mabon/* *Fall Equinox*	23	24	25	26	27	28
29	30					

Times are in Eastern Time.

2013
OCTOBER

SU	M	TU	W	TH	F	SA
		1	2	3	4 ● New Moon 8:35 pm	5
6	7	8	9	10	11	12
13	14 Columbus Day (observed)	15	16	17	18 🌝 Lunar Eclipse, Blood Moon, 7:38 pm	19
20	21	22	23	24	25	26
27	28	29	30	31 Samhain/ Halloween		

Times are in Eastern Time.

SU	M	TU	W	TH	F	SA
					1	2
					All Saints' Day	
3 ●	4	5	6	7	8	9
Solar Eclipse, New Moon 7:50 am *DST ends 2 am*		*Election Day (general)*				
10	11	12	13	14	15	16
	Veterans Day					
17 ☺	18	19	20	21	22	23
Mourning Moon, 10:16 am						
24	25	26	27	28	29	30
				Thanksgiving Day		

Times are in Eastern Time.

2013
DECEMBER

SU	M	TU	W	TH	F	SA
1	2 ● New Moon 7:22 pm	3	4	5	6	7
8	9	10	11	12	13	14
15	16	17 ☺ Long Nights Moon, 4:28 am	18	19	20	21 *Yule/* *Winter Solstice*
22	23	24 *Christmas Eve*	25 *Christmas Day*	26	27	28
29	30	31 *New Year's Eve*				

Times are in Eastern Time.

2014
JANUARY

SU	M	TU	W	TH	F	SA
			1 ● New Moon 6:14 am *New Year's Day*	2	3	4
5	6	7	8	9	10	11
12	13	14	15 ☺ Cold Moon 11:52 pm	16	17	18
19	20 *Martin Luther King, Jr. Day*	21	22	23	24	25
26	27	28	29	30 ● New Moon 4:39 pm	31	

Times are in Eastern Time.

2014
FEBRUARY

SU	M	TU	W	TH	F	SA
						1
2 *Imbolc/ Groundhog Day*	3	4	5	6	7	8
9	10	11	12	13	14 ☺ Quickening Moon, 6:53 pm *Valentine's Day*	15
16	17 *Presidents' Day (observed)*	18	19	20	21	22
23	24	25	26	27	28	

Times are in Eastern Time.

2014
MARCH

SU	M	TU	W	TH	F	SA
						1 ● New Moon 3:00 am
2	3	4	5	6	7	8
9 *DST begins 2 am*	10	11	12	13	14	15
16 ☺ Storm Moon 1:08 pm	17 *St. Patrick's Day*	18	19	20 *Ostara/ Spring Equinox*	21	22
23	24	25	26	27	28	29
30 ● New Moon 2:45 pm	31					

Times are in Eastern Time.

2014
APRIL

SU	M	TU	W	TH	F	SA
		1 *All Fools' Day*	2	3	4	5
6	7	8	9	10	11	12
13	14	15 ☺ Lunar Eclipse, Wind Moon, 3:42 am	16	17	18	19
20	21	22 *Earth Day*	23	24	25	26
27	28	29 ● Solar Eclipse, New Moon, 2:14 am	30			

Times are in Eastern Time.

SU	M	TU	W	TH	F	SA
				1	2	3
				Beltane		
4	5	6	7	8	9	10
11	12	13	14 ☺	15	16	17
Mother's Day			Flower Moon 3:16 pm			
18	19	20	21	22	23	24
25	26	27	28 ●	29	30	31
	Memorial Day (observed)		New Moon 2:40 pm			

Times are in Eastern Time.

2014
JUNE

SU	M	TU	W	TH	F	SA
I	2	3	4	5	6	7
8	9	IO	II	I2	I3 ☺ Strong Sun Moon, I2:II am	I4 Flag Day
I5 Father's Day	I6	I7	I8	I9	20	2I Litha/ Summer Solstice
22	23	24	25	26	27 ● New Moon 4:08 am	28
29	30					

Times are in Eastern Time.

2014
JULY

SU	M	TU	W	TH	F	SA
		1	2	3	4 Independence Day	5
6	7	8	9	10	11	12 ☺ Blessing Moon 7:25 am
13	14	15	16	17	18	19
20	21	22	23	24	25	26 ● New Moon 6:42 pm
27	28	29	30	31		

Times are in Eastern Time.

2014
AUGUST

SU	M	TU	W	TH	F	SA
					1	2
						Lammas
3	4	5	6	7	8	9
10 ☺	11	12	13	14	15	16
Corn Moon 2:09 pm						
17	18	19	20	21	22	23
24	25 ●	26	27	28	29	30
	New Moon 10:13 am					
31						

Times are in Eastern Time.

2014
SEPTEMBER

SU	M	TU	W	TH	F	SA
	1 *Labor Day*	2	3	4	5	6
7	8 ☺ Harvest Moon 9:38 pm	9	10	11	12	13
14	15	16	17	18	19	20
21	22 Mabon/ Fall Equinox	23	24 ● New Moon 2:14 am	25	26	27
28	29	30				

Times are in Eastern Time.

2014
OCTOBER

SU	M	TU	W	TH	F	SA
			1	2	3	4
5	6	7	8 ☺ Lunar Eclipse, Blood Moon, 6:51 am	9	10	11
12	13 Columbus Day (observed)	14	15	16	17	18
19	20	21	22	23 ● Solar Eclipse, New Moon, 5:57 pm	24	25
26	27	28	29	30	31 Samhain/ Halloween	

Times are in Eastern Time.

2014
NOVEMBER

SU	M	TU	W	TH	F	SA
						1 *All Saints' Day*
2 *DST ends 2 am*	3	4 *Election Day (general)*	5	6 ☺ Mourning Moon, 5:23 pm	7	8
9	10	11 *Veterans Day*	12	13	14	15
16	17	18	19	20	21	22 ● New Moon 7:32 am
23	24	25	26	27 *Thanksgiving Day*	28	29
30						

Times are in Eastern Time.

2014
DECEMBER

SU	M	TU	W	TH	F	SA
	1	2	3	4	5	6 ☺ Long Nights Moon, 7:27 am
7	8	9	10	11	12	13
14	15	16	17	18	19	20
21 ● New Moon 8:36 pm Yule/ Winter Solstice	22	23	24 Christmas Eve	25 Christmas Day	26	27
28	29	30	31 New Year's Eve			

Times are in Eastern Time.